LET THE CHURCH *be the*
CHURCH

LET THE CHURCH *be the*
CHURCH

Facing the Lack
of Moral Leadership
Accountability in
Christianity

BOBBY E. MILLS, PH.D.

NEW YORK

LET THE CHURCH *be the* CHURCH
Facing the Lack of Moral Leadership Accountability in Christianity

Published in New York, New York, by Morgan James Publishing. Morgan James and The Entrepreneurial Publisher are trademarks of Morgan James, LLC. www.MorganJamesPublishing.com

The Morgan James Speakers Group can bring authors to your live event. For more information or to book an event visit The Morgan James Speakers Group at www.TheMorganJamesSpeakersGroup.com.

BitLit
FOR ALL THE BOOKS YOU OWN

FREE eBook edition for your existing eReader with purchase

PRINT NAME ABOVE

For more information, instructions, restrictions, and to register your copy, go to www.bitlit.ca/readers/register or use your QR Reader to scan the barcode:

ISBN 978-1-61448-875-0 paperback
ISBN 978-1-61448-876-7 eBook
ISBN 978-1-61448-878-1 hardcover
Library of Congress Control Number:
2013947437

Cover Design by:
Rachel Lopez
www.r2cdesign.com

Interior Design by:
Bonnie Bushman
bonnie@caboodlegraphics.com

In an effort to support local communities, raise awareness and funds, Morgan James Publishing donates a percentage of all book sales for the life of each book to Habitat for Humanity Peninsula and Greater Williamsburg.

Get involved today, visit
www.MorganJamesBuilds.com

Habitat for Humanity®
Peninsula and
Greater Williamsburg
Building Partner

CONTENTS

ACKNOWLEDGMENTS

I wish to extend grateful appreciation and heartfelt thanks to highly respected personal friends for invaluable conversations about church, family, and society over the years. These spiritual discussions have informed the basis for the chapter discussions presented. Hence, grateful appreciation is extended to Dr. Robert E. Childress, pastor of Covenant Glen UMC, where I am a member; Pastor Raymond L. Farley, Greater New Sanctuary Baptist Church; Pastor John E. Cameron; Minister Lewis C. Parker Jr. of the Church of Christ; Minister James A. Young; and Minister Paul W. Smith. I am particularly grateful to Charles W. Moore for our spiritual friendship over many years of church, college/university, and political discussions and adventures.

Heartfelt appreciation is extended to Michelle Foreman, principal of Texas Serenity Academy Charter School, for her educational insights and Tammy Lanier, director of communications and public information at the Harris County Department of Education.

My college and university training at Friendship College, Barber-Scotia College, Colgate Rochester-Crozer Divinity School, the

University of Rochester, and Syracuse University was spiritually and academically impacted by the professors who invested ethical-moral capital in my professional development. My earnest prayer is that the recorded commentary will stand as a worthy dividend testimony to their greatness as scholarly and ethically moral professors. I am compelled to mention some by name: Dr. William P. Diggs; Dr. Dean H. Harper; Dr. Charles V. Willie, my professional-personal mentor; Dr. Howard F. Taylor, my doctoral dissertation advisor; Dr. Mark Abramson; Dr. Louis Kriesberg; Dr. William McCord; Dr. Gunther Remmling; Dr. Arlene Sukuma; and Dr. J. David Edelstein.

PREFACE

There is one Father, one Son (Jesus the Christ), and one Holy Spirit. Therefore, there should be one church: the church of Jesus Christ. Toward that end, Christians should come together and *let the church be the church*. In so doing, we become the people of God and above all *one nation under God*. To be sure, the answer to our many social-cultural problems is in the church of Jesus Christ—not at the barrel of guns, guns, and more guns. It is a truism: live by the sword, die by the sword. Human beings cannot kill the devil, only resist him, and of course he will depart from you. Therefore, Jesus is the answer because social-spiritual problems cannot be solved through guns. However, solutions can be found in *egalitarianism*, not in authoritarianism.

It has been rightly said that many are called but few are chosen. It is not within my power to question whether or not an individual has been called, but I can question whether or not an individual is *ready* because we judge trees by the fruit they bear. The same standard of judgment and measurement holds true for pastors. Hence, until pastors allow the church to be the church of Jesus Christ we will continue to have what comedian Flip Wilson described as the "church of what's happening now." It is ungodly to say "Lord, Lord" and appear to be running with the devil, because this is the epitome of double-mindedness and being confused.

How many churches do we need in a given community? How many churches do we need in a community for that community to be holy and whole? God's church creates unity not division; only churches of the world create division. Why then are there so many *different* churches in *all* neighborhoods?

Some pastoral leaders have formed an ungodly preaching style; they use preaching as a vehicle for personal material gain. Unfortunately, preaching has become in some instances a tool to emotionalize parishioners rather than spiritualize parishioners. Again, the objective of this preaching style is personal gain: material prosperity. In general, parishioners do not have problems with giving tithes and offerings; their major concerns are what the tithes and offerings are being spent on.

Some will invariably say that they have been blessed by the tenets of the prosperity gospel preached by some pastoral leaders. Of course, who's to say that this is not true? Because if God is for you who can be against you? "What then shall we say to these things? If God is for us, who is against us?" (Rom. 8:31). For we know that God should get the glory in all things, not the gospel of prosperity. On the one hand, we know that the *prosperity* of prosperity preachers comes from parishioners. While, on the other hand, the prosperity of parishioners does not come from prosperity-preaching pastors. The prosperity of parishioners comes from inheritance, hard work and self-sacrifice, the stock market, and winning the lottery.

The God who made the world and all things in it, since He is Lord of heaven and earth, does not dwell in temples made with hands; neither is He served by human hands, as though He needed anything, since He himself gives to all life and breath and all things: and He made from one, every nation of mankind to live on all the face of the earth, having determined their appointed times, and the boundaries of their habitation, that they should seek God, if perhaps they might grope for Him and find Him, though He is not far from each one of us. For in Him we live and move and exist, as even some of your own poets have said, for we also are His offspring. Being then the offspring of God, we ought not to think that the Divine Nature is like gold or silver or stone, an image formed by the art of man.

Acts 17:24–29

The institutional church should be the spiritual light that enlightens American society. The Christian story is about creation, the fall, spiritual redemption, and re-creation, not corporate individualistic money-making profits. This story is real: we are created in the spiritual image of God, and of course stories help us to make sense of reality.

America has a serious spiritual problem: from the church house to state Houses and especially the corridors of Washington, DC, America has a confused definition of leadership. God-fearing spiritual leadership is about a vision for love and service, not money making schemes (i.e., the collection plate).

The Christian church and its pastoral leadership have failed to morally lead America toward a more godly perfect union as the founding fathers had envisioned; therefore America is headed toward the abyss of immorality. Without a doubt, the overwhelming majority of young people from eighteen to thirty do not attend church at all. Consequently, these young people have virtually no abstract spiritual consciousness about the meaning of life—therefore they feel as though they are immortal; they do not fear God. They have been mechanized rather than spiritualized.

Fortunately the gospel, the good news, is that God is love—and love covers a multitude of sins.

If the church is to be the church, it must embrace Psalm 1: "Blessed is the man that walketh not in the counsel of the ungodly, nor standeth in the way of sinners, nor sitteth in the seat of the scornful. But his delight is in the Law of the Lord; and in his law doth he meditate day and night." Therefore, God plus one is a majority.

Jesus' ministry was about love and service; therefore the church's ministry ought to be about love and service. Jesus taught in parables, and he used the Good Samaritan story in order to illustrate his message about love and service (Luke 10:30–37).

The church is called to be the beacon along the side of the road, open to all to come as they are, for the remission and recapitulation of their soul's salvation, in order that one might grow in the grace and knowledge of our Lord and Savior Jesus Christ. The church is God's house of praise and prayer to the glory of Jesus Christ, not the house of money changers and thieves. To Him be the glory. "For we must all appear before the judgment seat of Christ; that everyone may receive the things done in his body; according to that he hath done, whether it be good or bad" (2 Cor. 5:10).

Our prayer is for spiritual unity, societal unity, and peace in all the churches of the saints (1 Cor. 14:33). For all things must be done decently and in order in all areas of communal life (1 Cor. 14:40). The *keys* to the kingdom of heaven are in the Bible, because Bible is an acronym for **b**asic **i**nstructions **b**efore **l**eaving **e**arth. Hence, as sure as you are here, you are going to leave. Where your soul goes is about free-will choice: heaven or hell. "And inasmuch as it is appointed for men to die once, and after this comes judgment" (Hebrews 9:27). My sincere prayer is that we allow the church to be the church of Jesus Christ our Lord and Savior and not the *church of what's happening now*. To God be the glory.

It is my sincere prayer that every reader will ask the following questions of this book:

- Is the commentary in this book based upon biblical truths?
- Is the commentary objective and fair, not emotional?
- Is the commentary oriented toward a more loving/just American society and world?
- Is the commentary beneficial to all concerned?

If the answer is yes to all four questions, then it is well with my soul and I have honored God.

PRAYER

Heavenly Father, by whose grace we live and have our being, we humbly pray that all Christians will let the institutional church be the spiritual church of Jesus Christ our Lord and Savior; and may it reign forever in our minds. Make us ever mindful, Father, that You made us and that we belong to You. But, more importantly, that when we walk through institutional church doors we enter giving You praise, glory, honor, and thanks. Bless Your name, because You are good and Your divine love is everlasting. We thank You, heavenly Father, for Your faithfulness because it endures from age to age and generation after generation. Let the church be the church. Amen!

INTRODUCTION

God's business is saving souls. God's method for saving souls is godly love and sacrificial service (benevolence): *servant leadership*. Without a doubt, God wants pastoral leaders who are willing to love and serve others in the name of His only begotten Son Jesus Christ, not self-serve. Indeed, Christians must allow the church to be the spiritual body of Jesus Christ, because God spiritually fixed the church in the Garden of Eden; because spiritually and symbolically the Garden of Eden was the church, therefore let the church be the church, and all Christian believers ought to say amen.

God did it: *Fixed the church*. Symbolically the Garden of Eden was God's church simply because everything Adam and Eve needed in order to experience heaven on earth was in the Garden of Eden, as expressed in the disciples' prayer commonly known as the Lord's Prayer. Likewise everything a believer needs should exist in the church of the twenty-first century. Unfortunately, too many double-minded pastors have ushered *hell* into church houses by not fully aligning themselves with God's spiritual purposes for the church, which is primarily soul salvation, not individualistic wealth creation.

If pastoral leaders will simply yield to the Holy Spirit—truth—God will add to the church of Jesus Christ. The Holy Spirit is what gives power to the church, not emotional-style preaching and staged productions with multimedia technology. On the one hand, God desires that we think and act with the logic of our minds, not our emotions. God is a logical God, not an emotional God. The devil desires that we think with our emotions rather than the logic of our minds for two reasons: he wants to break an individual down emotionally, and the best way to accomplish this objective is to get individuals to think with their emotions and orient life totally toward the flesh, or *carnal-mindedness*. The devil's objective is to make an individual become their own worst enemy because he knows that God is your best friend. He wants you to run from your moral issues/problems, not seek to solve them spiritually.

God desires that every individual break through to the spiritual truth about life, *not break down or break out*. He wants us to meet Him in partnership. This is why Christ-centered Christianity helps individuals develop high moral character and a pathway to soul salvation. Resist the devil and he will flee from you. The key to living a moral life is to know who gives the charge, not who is in charge. Double-minded pastors need to learn this profound spiritual lesson and stop getting hung up on the latter: who is in charge.

Of course, we should use twenty-first-century media technology to advance God's kingdom, but not abandon the Word of God (Bible) and His principles and instructional doctrines. In other words, Christianity should not become worldly-culture Christianity. "Therefore leaving the principles of the doctrine of Christ, let us go on unto perfection; not laying again the foundation of repentance from dead works, and of faith toward God" (Heb. 6:1). It is my heartfelt prayer that Christian leaders testify in the Word and walk in the Word: "For I rejoiced greatly, when the brethren came and testified of the truth that is in thee, even as thou walkest in the truth" (3 John 1:3).

To be sure, if you talk the talk you should be able to walk the walk. Jesus declared: "And I say unto thee, that thou art Peter, and upon this rock I will build my church; and the gates of hell shall not prevail against it" (Matt. 16:18). Pastoral leaders should remember that the only institution Jesus Christ is coming back for is *His* church, one without spot or wrinkle. In other words, in Matthew 16:18 Jesus acknowledges that hell will enter the church but *hellishness* shall not prevail against God's divine purpose for the church: (a) worship and praise, (b) meeting the spiritual (*soul salvation*) and material needs of the parishioners of the church, and (c) meeting the spiritual and material needs of the local communities in which churches exist. Preaching is preaching, but godly listening is altogether a different process. In my opinion, some pastoral leaders would desire that the church stand on *neutral* ground rather than *holy* ground.

Pastoral leaders should know that all of the preaching, moneymaking programs, and worldly entertainment hype, lying, and ungodly scheming will not produce a God-centered church, God-centered local neighborhoods, or a God-fearing society. All pastors should allow the church to be the church of Jesus Christ our Lord and Savior, and of course Jesus was extremely benevolent. God's name should not be taken in vain for personal gain, but there is no shame in some pastoral leaders' game. Without a doubt, God blesses through obedience to His divine will, because God rewards those who diligently seek Him (Heb. 11:1–6). God is not a divine Santa Claus. When obedience goes up heavenly blessings come down. Praising God and at the same time being disobedient to the will of God will not cause blessings to come down from heaven.

What then is preaching?

How do we get from institutional Christianity to spirituality?

These questions have plagued humankind from its inception. Even Jesus was confronted with this issue in the city of Jericho—and He had to shake the dust from His feet. A godly individual is always duty-bound to tell a *carnal-minded* individual the truth: "Thus says the Lord who made the heavens and earth and all that dwell therein." The Bible reminds us: "Do not lay hands upon anyone too hastily and thus share responsibility for the sins of others; keep yourself free from sin" (1 Tim. 5:22).

Preaching is what you say based upon the Word of God, not how you say it (preaching style). Preaching is explaining biblically based truths for the purpose of spiritualization, not emotionalizing.

Why are so many twenty-first-century pastors consistently calling for the re-crucifixion of Jesus and freeing of carnal-minded Barabbas, or the world? A Christian must be in the world but not of the world.

Pastors should preach the doctrine of Christ based upon biblical doctrine and not seek to become people pleasers, telling parishioners those things that simply turn their ears and hearts away from the truth.

Preaching is a command from God; therefore a pastor must be a man of (from) God, not the world. Before a pastor sells out he should get the hell out of the pulpit. Pastors must preach only the truth and hide behind the cross of Jesus Christ. I am reminded of a visiting pastor who was conducting a revival service for a pastoral friend. After his initial sermon a little old lady remarked to the pastor: "You something else." Each night for three nights in a row the little old lady made the same comments. On the fourth night when the little ole lady remarked, "You something else," the pastor asked, "Madam, for four nights you have uttered the same phrase. What do you mean?" The little old lady replied, "You are something else other than a pastor."

Second Peter 1:3–4 declares, "According as his divine power hath given unto us all things that pertain unto life and godliness, through the knowledge of him that hath called us to glory and virtue: Whereby are given unto us exceeding great and precious promises: that by these ye might be partakers of the divine nature, having escaped the corruption that is in the world through lust." The point being made here is that God desires that we enter into spiritual partnership with Him. Ecclesiastes 1:9–10 similarly declares, "The thing that hath been, it is that which shall be; and that which is done is that which shall be done: and there is no new thing under the sun. Is there anything whereof it may be said, See, this is new? It hath been already of old time, which was before us."

An appropriate adage comes to mind: "If it is new it's probably not true. If it's true it's probably not new." But, more importantly, God is good all the time, and for services in His spiritual kingdom building (heaven on earth), He pays well all the time.

Likewise the devil pays well—up front—in order to lure an individual into providing services to help him create *hellishness-confusion*, because at the end of the road you have personal destruction: *hell on earth*. An individual receives his reward upfront with the devil. This is one of the devil's biggest hooks. The devil's biggest hook is to use the weaker vessel: man or woman. The devil is not omnipresent and so he does not know what you are doing unless you tell him. This is precisely the reason why what goes on behind closed doors should remain behind closed doors. Closed doors are personal business and personal business is *personal*. For example, God made sexuality private activity between consenting adults in the Garden of Eden when He made lamb-skin coverings for Adam and Eve because of their disobedience. From disobedience (sin) covering must take place. Therefore, only you and God know what you are thinking or doing, because only God sees everything and knows everything. God created heaven by Himself but the devil needs help in order to create hell on earth. It is a truism that whosoever the gods first choose to destroy, they first make angry. Of course, the battle is the Lord's, and I have chosen to get in the fight for righteousness' sake (1 Sam. 17:47). It has rightly been said if you see a *righteous* fight going on for justice then join the fight. But if you see injustice and no one has started a *righteous* fight, then you start a righteous fight for justice, because justice is a spiritual concept.

The prophetic urgency of "NOW" is upon American pastoral leadership: "Come, and let us return unto the Lord: for he had torn, and he will heal us: he had smitten, and he will bind us up. After two days will he revive us: in the third day he will raise us up, and we shall live in his sight. Then shall we know, if we follow on to know the Lord: his going forth is prepared as the morning; and he shall come unto us as the rain, as the latter and former rain unto the earth" (Hos. 6:1–3).

American pastoral leaders should read 1 Timothy 6:6–7 daily as a constant reminder of their role as God's representatives, not self-representatives: "But godliness with contentment is great gain. For we brought nothing into this world, and it is certain we can carry nothing out." God's blessings are upon the head of the just, not the disobedient or wicked. "Blessings are upon the head of the just: but violence covereth the mouth of the wicked. The memory of the just is blessed: but the name of the wicked shall rot" (Prov. 10:6–7). Sometimes God's blessings come after we have experienced difficult times and remained faithfully obedient to God's will.

For example, Joseph was hated by his own biological brothers. In fact, they sold him into slavery. Eventually Joseph was sold to Potiphar, the chief of Pharaoh's bodyguards (Gen. 37:36). Because of Joseph's obedience to God, everything Joseph did met with success (Gen. 39:1–6). Potiphar's wife looked upon Joseph with sexual desire and wanted to lie with him. Joseph refused to lie with Potiphar's wife so she lied about him and had him thrown into prison. Pharaoh had a dream and none of his advisors could interpret the dream. So Pharaoh sent for Joseph, who explained the dream of both plenty and famine. Joseph told Pharaoh how to survive the famine (Gen. 41:1–36). Pharaoh realized that God's blessings were upon Joseph, and he promoted him from prisoner to governor of the kingdom, second only to Pharaoh himself (Gen. 41:1–36). The rest of the story is simply that what the devil meant for evil God meant for good.

Job also received God's blessings after difficult times, and he did not turn away from God even after being pressured to do so by his wife and trusted friends. He confessed his sins before God (Job 32:2). In the end, God restored Job to his former status and his life was blessed more at the end than it was at the beginning. Even his friends and relatives brought him gifts. When Job's obedience went up, heavenly blessings came down and he lived to see four generations of grandchildren (Job 42:16). That's the way it is, and that's the only way it is.

America is headed for the moral bankruptcy cliff because of the breakdown of the family unit, which is the foundation of society. The founding fathers envisioned America as the light of the world community, not the immoral standard of the world community. Name the sin and America can produce a shining example. To reiterate, society begins in the family unit. Society is not an abstraction, because the organization of society has real consequences. Unfortunately, secular society has sought to intellectualize greed. Institutional Christianity has sought to spiritualize greed based upon the teachings of the prosperity gospel. Both are unspiritual representations of God's will for His children. Greed is simply greed. Church begins in individual moral conscience and is instituted in the family unit. But, more importantly, the answer to societal chaos is in the institutional church of Jesus Christ, not the church of Joe Moe Blow. Christians must allow God to be God; then the church can be the church of Jesus Christ and the Holy Spirit can direct our individual and collective lives.

IT'S TIME FOR A NEW DIRECTION

The old guard cannot lead and of course they refuse to step aside. To be sure, where *spiritual ignorance* prevails people perish. For without a *spiritual vision* there is no future, and without God there is no such thing as a vision, because the future belongs to God. Of course, the search for spiritual understanding is neither easy nor popular.

American society is headed for the eternal bonfire simply because of the profound cultural lag that exists between church and society. It is a critical imperative that the church help usher in a godly standard of conduct for American culture whereby God is God, men are men, women are women, children are children, and the family is the family. Unfortunately the church is being led by secular culture rather than informing secular culture. Indeed, too many double-minded pastors are willing participants in this secularization of the church process—that is the church becoming worldly entertainment.

When this moral shift becomes a reality American society will have indeed changed directions and universal brotherhood under God will become a living reality. In the beginning there was one holy Trinity: God the Father, God the Son, and God the Holy Spirit. "And God said, Let us make man in our own image, after our likeness" (Gen. 1:26). The Godhead in three persons, blessed Trinity. Amen! "But as it is written, Eye hath not seen, nor ear heard, neither have entered into the heart of man, the things which God hath prepared for them that love him" (1 Cor. 2:9). Love God! Love God! Love God! Over time as mankind spiritually and mentally evolved he developed a *manmade* secular trinity oriented to help him understand the world as his natural habitat and, above all, his place in the scheme of things.

Now there are two trinities: a *divine Trinity* and a *worldly trinity*. The divine Trinity existed prior to the earth being formed. The *worldly trinity* (theology, sociology, and psychology—the *life of the mind*) is human invention and human understanding, or humankind attempting to make sense of its place in the scheme of things. "For as the heavens are higher than the earth, so are my ways higher than your ways, and my thoughts higher than your thoughts. For as the rain cometh down, and the snow from heaven, and returneth not thither, but watereth the earth, and maketh it bring forth and bud, that it may give seed to the sower, and bread to the eater: so shall my word be that goeth forth out of my mouth: it shall not return unto me void, but it shall accomplish that which I please, and it shall prosper in the thing whereto I sent it" (Isa. 55:9–11).

The holy Trinity is about godliness and soul salvation; it is about the first five commandments. The worldly trinity is about the second five commandments. This is precisely why Jesus reduced the Ten Commandments to the two great commandments: "Love God with all your heart, soul, and might and love your neighbor as yourself: Do unto others as you would have them do to you." Most of our civil and criminal codes are derived from the commandments.

The worldly trinity is in peril primarily because we have forgotten the first five commandments, especially the one about *idolatry*, and secondarily because of the breakdown of the family unit. Again, the worldly trinity is mankind's attempt to make sense out of his natural habitat—his relationship to nature as well as his relationship and interaction with each other. It is for this reason alone that there is a breakdown of our moral-spiritual relationship with God, not God's relationship with us, because God's relationship with us is a moral constant which has had untold societal consequences, especially for the family unit and education.

Society begins in the family, and therefore the breakdown of the family unit has devastating consequences on educational-spiritual development at every level. Educators cannot educate children that are not spiritually self-disciplined. Children who are not trained and taught the "way of the Lord" are usually not self-directed, self-motivated, or self-disciplined. The founding fathers thought it was essential that all citizens be able to read and write—in fact, read the Holy Bible. This is why a mass universal educational system was instituted. Democracy is virtually impossible without a mass universal education system and an intelligent citizenry.

Of course, universal spiritual family reunion will also become a reality. There is only *one church, one Savior,* and *one God,* and therefore denomination is abomination, because denominationalism is simply about *classism* and in some instances sexism and racism. The truth about human life is still simple even in the most affluent, technologically advanced nation on earth. The family is the school for God's love; godly love is the basis for community, so no true community exists without individuals embracing the reality of God.

For Jesus community was an unquestioned presupposition. Jesus walked along the shores of the Galilee with a revolutionary call, drawing men out of themselves and a livelihood of fishing for fish, or physical food. Jesus wanted to teach them how to use spiritual food to feed the souls of men and women. He asked these twelve men to learn how to fish for men—to save individual lives by learning how to feed them spiritual food. But, more importantly, He asked these twelve men to form a community under the *reality of God: the church.* In fact, Jesus and the twelve disciples were a family and at the same time the first Christian church, providing spiritual, emotional, and material support for each other. God gave us His best, Jesus. We should give each other our best because King David, a man after God's own heart and the apple of God's eye, declared: "I have been young, and now am old; yet have I not seen the righteous forsaken, nor his seed begging bread" (Ps. 37:25). We should give God our best because God gave us His best Jesus Christ, The Righteous One. The Baptism of Jesus is the confirmation of the facts. The social profoundness of the life of Jesus is that he had a talent (skill). He was a talented carpenter. All of the men He recruited had skills (talents). The spiritual profoundness of Christ (The Righteous One) was His ability to love and serve others as the gift of God. This is why the Gospel is free, the free Gift of God.

Therefore, the name Jesus represents humanity and the title Christ represents divinity.

> And Jesus answering said unto him, suffer it to be so now: *for thus it becometh us to fulfill all righteousness.* Then he suffered him. And Jesus, when he was baptized, went up straightway out of the water: and, lo the heavens were opened unto him, and he saw the Spirit of God descending like a dove, and lighting upon him: And lo a voice from heaven saying, This is my beloved Son, in whom I am well pleased.
>
> **Matthew 3:15–17**

There is a destiny that makes us one. No individual goes his or her own way. All ways are interconnected. What we invest in the lives of others comes back into our own. Individualistic or materialistic religion is not the answer to acquiring peace of mind, which in turn is what *joy,* is all about. Joy is not modernistic, capitalistic materialism. What then is joy? In many profound ways the Bible declares that to be broke and not have any worries is joy. The classical biblical example of joy is the story of Peter and John in the book of Acts (3:1–10), healing the lame beggar at the gate of the Temple. Peter told the beggar: "Silver and gold I do not have, but such as I have I give to you: In the name of Jesus Christ of Nazareth rise up and walk." The man leaped to his feet and ran into the Temple praising God.

To the lame beggar joy was healing; he forgot about not having money (silver and gold). He probably went to work. Without a doubt, what we invest in the lives of others comes back into our own because God cares and He never fails. God can do anything but fail. Someone told me to deliver this message, and I am sure you know who you are. I sincerely hope that lay Christians, biblical scholars, and theologians will enjoy reading the message presented here.

The emphasis of this book is to engage lay Christians in the work of Jesus' Great Commission, soul saving, because many Christians have the right approach but the wrong spiritual doctrine. The Bible is condensed godly history, and all righteousness and spiritual understanding is recorded in the Bible. "But these are written, that ye might believe that Jesus is the Christ, the Son of the living God; that believing ye might have life through his name" (John 20:31). "And this is life eternal, that they might know thee the only true God, and Jesus Christ, whom thou hast sent" (John 17:3).

It is my sincere hope that the socio-religious commentary recorded here will represent a lasting down-payment on the spiritual healing process in American society in particular and Western societies in general. Each chapter ends with a specific prayer. Prayer changes things! Therefore, it is my earnest prayer that readers might experience positive change and become better for having read *Let the Church Be the Church*.

The chapters were selected based upon their interdependent and interrelational spiritual nature to each other: God, family, church, education, society, and political governance. Increasingly, America has developed a serious God problem and spiritual problem. The basis for human existence and human relationships is God and His Word, the Holy Bible. Questions emerge: What is God's divine purpose for bringing and keeping order in the creation and universe? What is God's divine purpose for creating human beings? His purpose for creation is the fourfold positional foundation as recorded in Genesis: be spiritually fruitful, multiply/procreate, replenish (do not abuse the environment), and lastly subdue the earth by maintaining order under the authority and power of God.

We were not to allow the prince of the air, the devil, either to influence us or rule over the earth and environment.

And you hath he quickened, who were dead in trespasses and sins: wherein in time past ye walked according to the course of this world, according to the prince of the power of the air, the spirit that now worketh in the children of the disobedience: among whom also we all had a conversation in times past in the lusts of the flesh and of the mind; and were by nature the children of wrath, even as others.

Ephesians 2:1–3

Adam's spiritual power was to name everything in the Garden of Eden. How did Adam know that a dog was a dog, a cow was a cow, and so forth? He had not seen these animals before. It seems obvious that Adam received the names through spiritual consciousness from God—where else? The devil cannot create, only confuse and destroy. Therefore, Adam's role was to dress and keep the Garden of Eden. Then God made a help-meet for Adam: Eve. Eve's role was to help Adam meet his spiritual obligation to God. So we see that the basis for establishing a righteous society is God and His Word, not the prince of the air, the devil. God has declared that where two or three are gathered together in the name of Jesus, He will be in the midst of them. God is not in the midst of confusion. My purpose is to simply remind every Christian believer that God is not fooled nor is He mocked; every individual reaps what he or she sows.

Without a doubt, each individual has a soul appointment with a living God that cannot be canceled. Individuals can cancel appointments with doctors, dentists, business associates, and personal friends, but each of us has a *soul appointment* with a living God that cannot be canceled.

PRAYER

God of our fathers, we humbly pray that all may come to know the path of life and in Thy presence find love, joy, hope, and peace evermore. In so doing, we pray that all individuals learn how to climb Jacob's ladder to heaven. Heavenly Father, we ask for Your guidance in all that we think, say, and do. But most of all we pray that our character and intellectual integrity be free from the love of money because You have promised never to leave us fatherless. For it is recorded that neither the righteous nor the seed of the righteous shall beg for bread. We know, heavenly Father, that the earth might pass away but Your WORD will stand. In the priceless name of Jesus we humbly pray. Let the church be the church. Get right, church. The King of Kings is coming. Amen!

GOD

God is God and besides Him there is none other.

Exodus 33:17

LET GOD BE GOD

Hear, O Israel: The Lord our God is one Lord: And thou shalt love the Lord thy God with all thine heart, and with all thy soul, and with all thy might. And these words, which I command thee this day, shall be in thine heart: and thou shalt teach them diligently unto thy children, and shalt talk of them when thou sitteth in thine house, and when thou walkest by the way, and when thou liest down, and when thou riseth up.

Deuteronomy 6:4–7

1

To be sure, what individuals think about God determines what they think about themselves, others, duty, responsibility, and most of all human destinies. There is a higher spiritual reality. Reality is not just what individuals see with their physical eyes. The Hebrew prophet Ezekiel declared that looking up he saw a big wheel in the middle of a wheel in the middle of a wheel. But after another look he saw a little bitty wheel in the midst of all the big wheels—it was the reality of God making all the big wheels go around.

Of course, some people actually disbelieve in God. Atheists are usually individuals who are in rebellion against some unworthy ideas about God. Every human being is confronted with one central life-changing question: who do you love more, the Giver or the gifts? For "Every good and perfect gift is from above, and cometh down from the Father of lights, with whom is no variableness, neither shadow of turning" (James 1:17). Of course, the devil gives gifts too; however the devil's gifts are from the pit of hell because they are illusory. "Love not the world, neither the things that are in the world, if any man love the world, the love of the Father is not in him. For all that is in the world, the lust of the flesh, and the lust of the eyes, and the pride of life, is not of the Father, but is of the world" (1 John 2:15–16).

This is why what is God to some is the devil to others. Indeed, this is also why Job cried: "Oh, that I knew where I might find Him" (Job 23:3). While on the other hand the psalmist celebrates the inescapable presence of God through a poem:

O Lord, thou hast searched me, and known me. Thou knowest my down sitting and mine uprising, thou understandest my thoughts afar off. Thou compassest my path and my lying down, and are acquainted with all my ways. For there is not a word in my tongue, but, lo, O Lord, thou knowest it altogether. Thou hast beset me behind and before, and laid thine hand upon me. Such knowledge is too wonderful for me; it is too high. I cannot attain unto it. Wither shall I go from thy spirit? Or whither shall I flee from thy presence? If I ascend up into heaven, thou art there: if I make my bed in hell, behold, thou art there. If I take the wings of the morning, and dwell in the utter most parts of the sea; even there shall thy hand lead me, and thy right hand shall hold me.

Psalm 139:1–10

GOD IS NOT CHAINED TO AN ALTAR

God is not localized; He travels with individuals and therefore reveals Himself universally. So every individual is without excuse.

The psalmist celebrates free will, freedom of mind that God gives to every individual soul. It goes without saying that this psalm is indeed cherished by children of God. Its truth has a cutting edge, a truth that is not proven by scientific logic but by positive interdependent living. Human beings were created to be in fellowship-partnership with God and with each other. The mind that seeks to escape from the reality of God always finds it impossible to do so, because God is the reality of absolute *truth*.

The absolute truth is that individuals did not give life to themselves. If that were the case—if individuals could create themselves—then most sane-minded people would not physically die but live in physical form forever. "In the beginning was the Word, and the Word was with God, and the Word was God. The same was in the beginning with God. All things were made by him; and without him was not anything made that was made. In him was life; and the life was the light of men" (John 1:1–3).

Who is God? What is reality? God is an axiomatic given, inherently untestable, and therefore God is not a problem to be solved but a *spiritual force* to be joined. God's wisdom is above humankind's knowledge and understanding. God's thoughts and ways are not like those of humanity. "For my thoughts are not your thoughts, neither are your ways my ways, saith the Lord. For as the heavens are higher than the earth, so are my ways higher than your ways, and my thoughts than your thoughts" (Isa. 55:8–9).

The creation story tells the whole story. In order to escape God individuals must deny selfhood—that is, deny what is since individuals did not create themselves and cannot keep themselves from experiencing physical death. But they do not have to experience spiritual death. The devil can only exercise his gifts when he is able to get permission from a host-body since he is not omnipresent like God.

Eve gave the devil permission to exercise his gifts of deception, distortion, lies, trickery, and confusion. In order to work his will the devil must first get an individual to cut off his/her conscience from the reality of God, because God only deals with individuals through moral conscience. When individuals cut off conscience from God, they are without God. This is why the devil was able to exercise his gifts in the Garden of Eden through Eve. Therefore the church was corrupted and Jesus came to restore the church; the very gates of hell shall not prevail against God's soul salvation plan. In American society those who seek to escape from the *reality of God* are best described as truth-dodgers or lie-accommodators rather than ideological atheists.

God is the Maker (Creator) of all things. God demands righteousness and He desires our worship and praise. Because, "The Lord is my light and my salvation; whom shall I fear? The Lord is the strength of my life; of whom shall I be afraid? When the wicked, even mine enemies and my foes, came upon me to eat up my flesh, they stumbled and fell" (Ps. 27:1–2). Furthermore, "I will bless the Lord at all times: his praise shall continually be in my mouth. My soul shall make her boast in the Lord: the humble shall hear thereof, and be glad" (Ps. 34:1–2). Moreover, "A thousand shall fall at thy side, and ten thousand at thy right hand; but it shall not come nigh thee. Only with thine eyes shalt thou behold and see the reward of the wicked" (Ps. 91:7–8). Therefore, God's delight is in our obedience to His will. *Self-righteousness is devilish*, because "For as by one man's disobedience many were made sinners, so by the obedience of one shall many be made righteous" (Rom. 5:19).

"What shall we say then? Shall we continue in sin, that grace may abound? God forbid. How shall we, that are dead to sin, live any longer therein" (Rom. 6:1–2)? All leaders both spiritual as well as political should heed God's warning: "For the leaders of this people cause them to err; and they that are led of them are destroyed. Therefore, the Lord shall have no joy in their young men, neither shall have mercy on their fatherless and widows; for everyone is a hypocrite and an evildoer, and every mouth speaketh folly. For all this his anger is not turned away, but his hand is stretched out still" (Isa. 9:16–17).

Even in the midst of profound wickedness God's desire is human *restoration*. Jesus says, "Come unto me, all ye that labor and are heavy laden, and I will give you rest. Take my yoke upon you, and learn of me; for I am meek and lowly in heart: and ye shall find rest unto your souls. For my yoke is easy, and my burden light" (Matt. 11:28–30). The Jesus way is the *only* way because it is God's divine salvation plan for His children. "For if these things be in you, and abound, they make you that ye shall neither be barren nor unfruitful in the knowledge of the Lord Jesus Christ. But he that lacketh these things is blind, and cannot see afar off, and hath forgotten that he was purged from his old sins" (2 Pet. 1:8–9).

"Praise ye the Lord. Blessed is the man that feareth the Lord that delighteth greatly in his commandments. His seed shall be mighty upon the earth: the generation of the upright shall be blessed. Wealth and riches shall be in his house: and his righteousness endureth forever" (Ps. 112:1–4).

God that made the world and all things therein, seeing that he is the Lord of heaven and earth, dwelleth not in temples made with hands; neither is worshipped with men's hands, as though he needed anything, seeing he giveth to all life, and breath, and all things; and he hath made of one blood all nations of men for to dwell on all the face of the earth, and hath determined the times before appointed, and the bounds of their habitation; that they should seek the Lord, if haply they might feel after him, and find him, though he be not far from every one of us. For in him we live, and move and have our being; as certain also of your own poets have said, for we are also his offspring. Forasmuch then as we are the offspring of God, we ought not to think that the Godhead is like unto gold, or silver, or stone, graven by art and man's device. And the times of this ignorance God winked at; but now commandeth all men everywhere to repent; because he hath appointed a day, in which he will judge the world in righteousness by that man he hath ordained whereof he hath given assurance unto all men, in that he hath raised him from the dead.

Acts 17:24–31

There are three important ideas embodied in this passage of Scripture. Foremost is the idea that individuals must worship God with their minds (human will and conscience), and of course just as important is the idea that the earth is humankind's natural habitat. Our souls are housed in our minds. Let the mind that was in Christ Jesus be also in you, which in turn is the *mind of God*. But, more importantly, the perfection of God is clearly expressed in the fact that God has no physical needs because He is *perfect in love*. The needy invariably become the greedy. God confronts every individual with this ultimate question: who do you love more, the *Giver* or the *gift*? Individuals who have enormous needs are rarely ever satisfied. Neediness engenders insecurity and insecurity creates the need to exploit others.

Self-control and self-discipline are indeed difficult character traits to acquire (God, of course, is completely self-sufficient). In my opinion, to learn to rely totally upon one's *own spirit force* is paradoxically to learn to rely on the Spirit of God. That is, the power within. Jesus always referred to the Kingdom of God being within, rather than without. Hence, to know the power of self is to know the power of God. Again, in my opinion direct knowledge of self is indirect knowledge of God. Unfortunately, most individuals culturally learn to deal with self negatively because they learn to define themselves by external characteristics (categories) rather than internal moral character traits, and consequently they deal with God negatively. *Self is the enemy.*

The essential character of God is freedom. God is not an authoritarian dictator of human will, or mindset. God's vision is for *all* to behold: "look up with the eyes of your mind, not your physical eyes, and indeed you will see a higher reality." Without a doubt, reality has two dimensions: (1) reality as appearance and (2) reality as truth—it is what it is. In many situations perception is greater than the truth. However, things are not always what they seem to be. Everything that looks like gold is not gold: all gold does not glitter. Even unpolished diamonds do not glitter. There are *many* diamonds in the rough. Therefore, reality is not always appearance. The story of Ezekiel's experience with a wheel in the middle of a wheel is an applicable analogy of the reality of God (Ezek. 1:16–21).

It is easier for an individual to believe a lie than the truth because a lie only requires belief-rhetoric, but an individual has to work to discover the truth. *Truth is what it is, because God is who He is all by Himself.* Absolute truth and God are synonymous. With God it is about faith, not physical sight. Hence, God is the author and finisher of goodness and the devil enlists humans to help him become the author and finisher of evil and confusion. Human failures are not God's failures: God can do anything but fail. Without a doubt, positive fear of God is wisdom and of course to abandon evil is understanding. "Wise men lay up knowledge: but the mouth of the foolish is near destruction" (Prov. 10:14).

Individuals seek to "relativize" the truth in order to deny the authority of God over life. The earth is the Lord's and the fullness thereof, and all that dwell therein. Of course, many societies seek to institutionalize lies—that is lock the truth out of their institutional structures and social processes in order to exploit certain individuals. Indeed, the "dereliction" god-complex of some individuals causes them to deny the existence of absolute truth. Playing God is a dangerous game, but this is precisely what is wrong with *some* people, trying to become something they can never be: Godlike but not God. Therefore individuals should be what they are in God, not seek to play God.

Truth defines and a lie(s) deludes and creates confusion. To accept absolute truth then is to accept the centrality of God's will and therefore to accept egalitarianism rather than authoritarianism. There are no gods on earth, only finite human beings; Godlike but not God. "But the Lord is the true God; He is the living God, and an everlasting king: at his wrath the earth shall tremble, and the nations shall not be able to abide his indignation. Thus shall ye say unto them, the gods that have not made the heavens and the earth, even they shall perish from the earth, and from under these heavens. He hath made the earth by his power, he hath established the world by his wisdom, and hath stretched out the heavens by his discretion" (Jer. 10:10–12).

God is the *primal energy* source from which everything in the universe derives energy for life. The human body is formed, like all other material bodies, of electrons and atoms. These electrons and atoms are in perpetual motion and are governed by invisible yet definite universal laws. Indeed, everything in the universe operates according to cyclical principles. Material manifestations are projections of primal energy (God), the invisible source of all power. For example, the paper that this book is printed on was an invisible idea before it was a material manifestation. God is a spiritual source of power, and of course His kingdom is a spiritual kingdom, not a material kingdom.

God's kingdom does not come in and of itself. God's kingdom is about humankind's inner spirit toward self and neighbor. The decline of the idea of God as a *moral absolute* in American society has produced the privatization (individuation) and commercialization of Christianity. Whatever else religion/Christianity is, it is foremost a group phenomenon. Individuals attend churches as families and groups and, more importantly, they worship as a group. However, an individual must experience the *reality of God* individually but most of all come to know God in the pardoning and forgiveness of his or her sins.

To be sure, moral bankruptcy engenders a despair of intellectual integrity and moral character; and of course despair creates a sense of hopelessness. There is a striking contradiction between what God is and what we as Americans *are becoming*, what God demands and what we choose to do, and most of all, God's spiritual church and humankind's institutional Christian church. Of course, the world will always stand at attention for those who have maturity of spiritual purpose and a positive vision direction for the future.

God is not some kitchen shelf of illusions about life that blinds individuals to truth and ultimate reality. God is the only unifying force in the world as it is or the world as it shall be, because God is absolute truth. Hence, *God is not Santa Claus*; He is a rational ontological spiritual being, logical to the *nth* degree. God does not give blessings (*gifts*) and expect nothing in return. God is LIFE. Religion is a way of life, and therefore God is not a negative crutch but a positive force for positive *self-talk*. Every individual is born into this world as God's truth, not another individual's lie. To be what we are in Christ (*righteousness*) then is the real challenge in human existence. Therefore, truth is a powerful defense system. To learn to consistently rule over one's own spirit is the essence of creative religious living. Great then is the individual who consciously kills the self of today in order that he/she might live today, tomorrow, and spiritually forever.

Conceptually, the Judeo-Christian idea of God is in radical opposition to twenty-first-century institutional Christian practices. In the Old Testament God is the only hero, the *Lawgiver*. He travels with individuals because He is not chained to a sacred altar or housed in a physical temple, tent, or twenty-first-century mega-church sanctuary. God is rational and logical. The harmony in nature expresses the rationality and harmony of God. Without a doubt, the institutional practices of twenty-first-century Christian churches are radically different from what God demands as expressed in the precepts, teachings, and examples of Jesus Christ.

Deuteronomy 8:11 warns us against forgetting God. "Beware that thou forget not the Lord thy God, in not keeping his commandments, and his judgments, and his statutes, which I command this day." Therefore, fear of God is the beginning of knowledge, but fools despise wisdom and instruction.

Blessed is the man that walketh not in the counsel of the ungodly, nor standeth in the way of sinners, nor sitteth in the seat of the scornful. But his delight is in the law of the Lord; and in his law doth he mediate day and night. And he shall be like a tree planted by the rivers of water, that bringeth forth his fruit in his season; his leaf also shall not wither; and whatsoever he doeth shall prosper. The ungodly are not so: but are like the chaff which the wind driveth away. Therefore the ungodly shall not stand in the judgment, nor sinners in the congregation of

the righteous. For the Lord knoweth the way of the righteous:
but the way of the ungodly shall perish.

Psalm 1:1–5

God's fourfold foundational plan is His absolute truth about the meaning of human existence and His divine soul-salvation plan. Of course, for a moment the devil threw a monkey wrench in the salvation plan.

In Genesis 1:27–28 God gives the *fourfold positional foundation* for humankind to experience *heaven on earth, or godly living*: "So God created man in his *own* image, in the image of God created he him, male and female created he them. And God blessed them, and God said unto them, be fruitful, and multiply, and replenish the earth, and subdue it: and have dominion over the fish of the sea and over the fowl of the air, and over every living thing that moveth upon the earth."

God created both man and woman in His spiritual image; neither is to have dominion over the other. It is imminently clear why God made sure the *man* (Adam) had nothing to do with the *making* of a woman (Eve). *Adam was in a deep sleep.* A man is required to love a woman, not seek to *physically* rule over a woman. "So ought men to love their wives as their own bodies. He that loveth his wife loveth himself. For no man ever yet hated his own flesh; but nourisheth and cherisheth it, even as the Lord the church" (Eph. 5:27–29). Hence, a woman's existence just like that of a man is grounded in the *spiritual reality of God*. Therefore, both Adam and Eve are at the pinnacle of God's creation. God created Eve as Adam's *help-meet* in order that he might be able to meet his moral obligation (duty) to God.

Human beings were created to glorify God. Hence, what we think about God influences what we think about ourselves as humans, duty, and our infinite obligation to each other. The Garden of Eden was where God met with Adam and Eve in spiritual partnership, just as God meets with us in spiritual partnership in the church of the twenty-first century (if we permit Him to do so). The only difference is that Adam and Eve were sinless, and there was no sin in the Garden of Eden. Not so with the institutional church of today. Everyone brings sin to the institutional church, and foremost pastors. Even the New Testament writer Paul declared "I am chief among all sinners." The Garden of Eden was so pure that God Himself visited Adam and Eve there.

God's first instructional command to Adam and Eve was to be spiritually fruitful as *individuals—that is for them to experience spiritual completeness on an individual level: self-development*. Learning to rule over one's own spirit is the essence of spiritual completeness and maturity. It has been said, "To thine own self be true." Humans, not animals, are conscious of the meaning of physical death, and of course this is essentially why we can understand morality and moral conscience. To be sure, the basis for morality is God: *absoluteness*. Consequently, we are aware that there is a part of us as humans called *soul* that does not die. If Adam and Eve had experienced spiritual completeness on an individual level they would have fully understood their obligation to God and to each other. Without a doubt, Adam and Eve were spiritually immature because of the devil's intervention tactic, and therefore they could not be true to the *Truth* (God) and *likewise be true to self or each other.*

Spiritual understanding (*wisdom*) and intellectual integrity is the beginning of everything. Of course, when we have spiritual understanding as human beings everything else is in order because we say what we mean and we mean what we say. Jesus put it best when He said, "If you do not believe me for what I say, believe me for my works' sake." King Solomon said it best: "Get wisdom, get understanding: forget it not; neither decline from the words of my mouth" (Proverbs 4:5). The spiritual key is to have an understanding of wisdom because it forms the foundation of your soul salvation.

Secondly, God told Adam and Eve to *multiply*, and of course Adam and Steve cannot multiply. *Multiply* simply means each animal species reproduces after its own kind. Hence, multiply is about family and children. Marriage is about children: procreation. The concept of same-sex marriage is about vanity-seeking pleasure.

Since we are essentially spiritual beings housed in physical bodies, the objective is not to reproduce *spiritual immaturity but spiritual maturity*. Is this not what children bearing children is all about: *spiritual immaturity*? First Peter 2:1–5 declares: "Wherefore laying aside all malice, and all guile, and hypocrisies, and envies, and all evil speakings, as newborn babies, desire the sincere milk of the word, that ye may grow thereby: if so be ye have tasted the Lord is gracious. To whom coming, as unto a living stone, disallowed indeed of men, but chosen of God, and precious, ye also as lively stones, are built up a spiritual house, a holy priesthood, to offer up spiritual sacrifices, acceptable to God by Jesus Christ."

Likewise the New Testament writer Paul says: "And I, brethren, could not speak unto you as unto spiritual, but as unto carnal, even as unto babes in Christ. I have fed you with milk, and not meat: for hitherto ye were not able to bear it, neither yet now are ye able. For ye are yet carnal: for whereas there is among you envying, and strife, and divisions, are ye not carnal, and walk as men?" (1 Cor. 3: 1–3). These scriptures enlighten us as to why God commanded Adam and Eve to grow in fellowship with self (*self-spiritual development*), each other, and ultimately with Him. Of course, the devil tricked Eve into violating God's fourfold positional foundation divine plan. God asked Adam and Eve: who told you that you were naked?

To be sure, the devil desires to see every individual *naked and indecent* before God, that is with no conscience. Multiply means having offspring (children). Each animal species was ordained to reproduce after its own kind. Before Adam and Eve experienced the *process* of reproduction God married them in the Garden of Eden, the church. Spiritually, therefore, *illegitimate parents* are the central moral problem in American society, not illegitimate children. Parents are the examples for children just as pastors should be the example(s) to parishioners. For after all, example is the best teacher. Jesus was a worthy teacher because He was an example of His own teaching. Jesus lived by every word that came forth from His own mouth. Many pastors boldly declare that parishioners should live by every word that comes out of the Lord's mouth. Unfortunately, too many pastors do not live by the words that come out of their own mouths.

Thirdly, God commanded that Adam and Eve replenish the earth. Truth creates and a lie destroys. An individual can only create and replenish with the truth, not a lie. In other words, do not create an environmental crisis that will destroy humanity as well as consume the earth with wildfires, floods, and all sorts of natural disasters. Replenish means to restore, that is spiritually respect God's creation, for the earth is the Lord's and the fullness thereof. Adam and Eve were to "fill" the earth with people and animals, occupy the whole earth, and maintain harmony in the creation. They were commanded to keep the earth in *divine order*. God's desire was that Adam and Eve exercise self-control and self-discipline that they might become *godly* stewards and efficient caretakers of the earth.

From the beginning of time God has always had laws and principles, and of course He does not take away the right of an individual to do wrong. But God will never violate His own laws or principles. God told Adam and Eve, "If you follow My Word [*commandments, instructions*] I will lead you step-by-step into creating heaven on earth; and therefore you will be able to reproduce, replenish, restore, and respect the earth as your natural habitat."

Therefore everything must be under the subjection of God.

According as his divine power hath given unto us all things that pertain unto life and godliness, through the knowledge of him that hath called us to glory and virtue: Whereby are given unto us exceeding great and precious promises: that through these ye might be partakers of the divine nature, having escaped the corruption that is in the world through lust. And beside this, giving all diligence, add to your faith virtue; and to virtue knowledge; and to knowledge temperance; and to temperance patience, and to patience godliness; and to godliness brotherly kindness; and to brotherly kindness charity. For if these be in you, and abound, they make you that ye shall neither be barren nor unfruitful in the knowledge of our Lord Jesus Christ.

1 Peter 1:3–8

God's gift of free will gives every individual the ability to develop self-discipline, self-control, and self-knowledge—these are the keys to ruling over one's own spirit. Charity is the greatest virtue because charity is about love and service to one's fellowman. This scripture provides basic instructions for *godly living* before leaving this earth. While the earth is our *natural habitat*, it is not our eternal home since we are essentially spiritual beings. Without a doubt, we have a home that is not built by human hands.

Fourthly, God commanded that Adam and Eve subdue the earth, not subdue each other. By subdue God meant keep the earth under *godly influence and control*. In order to do so Adam and Eve needed *spiritual self-control*. To be sure, the devil has been working overtime— even working the night shift—to bring the earth under his influence (authority) and I might add thus far succeeding in his efforts. Of course, the devil's illusion is that sin does not bring about death. God hates sin; therefore the wages of sin is death, spiritually as well as physically. Thus, to have spiritual self-control an individual must possess *godliness*.

Children of children seek to play at being God rather than learn how to be what they are in God—children of God, not God. The devil's Garden of Eden trick created disharmony, and since that time humans have been seeking to subdue one another through "isms": *sexism, racism, classism, communism,* and so on.

Hence, all "isms" are indeed schisms and ultimately separate us from the love of God that was in Jesus Christ reconciling the world unto God and individuals unto each other. Charity is what keeps hope alive, and of course charity is simply godly love and service (action). Telling someone that you love them is not as important as showing love through action. Love is an action word; faith is also action. But faith without works is dead. "Even so faith, if it has not works, is dead, being alone" (James 2:17). Humans are in control of the earth, and God commanded Adam and Eve to dress and keep the Garden of Eden. Today the Garden of Eden is the earth as we know it. As Christians, we have missed the mark because we have been undressing (*destroying*) the earth as well as undressing each other, rather than dressing.

Cain was the first seed of Adam and Eve, and seemingly all unrighteousness came from Cain because he lied to God. When God asked Cain "Where is Abel thy brother?" he answered: *"Am I my brother's keeper?"* Nowhere in Scripture is it recorded that *Cain died.* John 8:44 declares: "Ye are of your father the devil, and the lusts of your father ye will do. He was a murderer from the beginning, and abode not in the truth, because there is no truth in him. He speaketh a lie, he speaketh of his own: for he is a liar and the father of it." God is TRUTH and the devil is a LIE; therefore the beginning of sin is also a *lie.*

Romans 15:4 emphatically declares: "For whatsoever things were written aforetime were written for our learning, that we through patience and comfort of scriptures might have hope." *Love is what keeps hope alive.* The four seasons will always exist simply because *God is God.* The imbalance in nature, just like the imbalance in American society, is of our own doing simply because we have failed to love God and to love each other as God has commanded. Instead we have done exactly the opposite of what God commanded us to do: "Beloved, let us love one another: for love is of God; and everyone that loveth is born of God, and knoweth God. He that loveth not knoweth not God; for God is love" (1 John 4:7–8).

As Christians, we are not to love the world or the things in the world since we have a home not built by human hands. Psalm 20:7 states it plainly: "Some trust in chariots, and some in horses, but we will remember the name of the Lord our God." Unfortunately, too many double-minded pastors are not under the subjection of the Word of God, because the Word of God is a two-edged sword. The truth cuts both ways, impacting both the *teller* and the *receiver.*

Too many double-minded pastors are not preaching to spiritualize parishioners toward heavenly things, but rather emotionalizing toward earthly materialistic concerns based upon the collection plate.

> I charge thee therefore before God, and the Lord Jesus Christ, who shall judge the quick and the dead at his appearing and his kingdom; preach the word; be instant in season, out of season; reprove, rebuke, exhort with all longsuffering and doctrine. For the time will come when they will not endure sound doctrine; but after their own lusts shall they heap to themselves teachers, having itching ears; and they shall turn away their ears from the truth, and shall be turned unto fables. But watch thou in all things, endure afflictions, do the work of an evangelist, make full proof of thy ministry.
>
> **2 Timothy 4:1**

Preaching is not a job; it is a *divine commitment* that an individual makes to God. Too many churches are not helping to keep *pastors* and *churchgoers* under the subjection of God's Word: biblical authority. Simply put, too many so-called Christians have drifted away from God's way. "Therefore, to one who knows the right thing to do good, and does not do it, to him it is sin" (James 4:17).

It is our Christian duty to do the right thing, not to do evil. "But I say unto you which hear, Love your enemies, do good to them that hate you, bless them that curse you, and pray for them which despitefully use you" (Luke 6:27–28). America's beginning was grounded in godly precepts recognizing that our human rights come from God, not civil authority. Most of these men were troubled in their very souls over the issue of chattel slavery. Thomas Jefferson was so vexed over the issue that he wanted to include a clause in the Constitution objecting to chattel slavery.

In fact, America's founding fathers were God-centered men who desired that American society's governmental philosophy embody God-centered principles and values: the doctrine of Jesus Christ. They established a governmental system based upon the concept of *one nation under God indivisible with liberty and justice for all.* In many of his writings George Washington refers to God as the benign *parent* (father/mother) of the human race. Even though many of the founding fathers owned slaves, in their *estate wills* they decreed that their slaves should be freed because they did not want their souls to confront God's judgment having enslaved other humans. Their desire was not a theocracy but a righteous society based upon the *separation of church and state* doctrine. For after all, justice is a spiritual concept. Indeed, a nation divided against itself cannot stand. "But seek ye first the kingdom of God, and his righteousness; and all these things shall be added unto you" (Matt. 6:33). Seeking God and embracing godliness creates societal unity: first things first. Righteousness exalts a society.

These God-fearing men understood that the *lure of loving money* presented a problem for both individuals as well as society. In fact, the founding fathers knew that money was a cruel master. "No man can serve two masters: for either he will hate the one, and love the other; or else he will hold to the one, and despise the other. Ye cannot serve God and mammon" (Matt. 6:24). Therefore, inscribed on American currency are these profound words: "In God We Trust." The inscription of these words on our currency is no accident of human history. Unfortunately, over time too many Americans have been lured into believing that money is indeed *god*, and they have placed their hope, ultimate trust, and love in the things of this world.

Money is not an answer to all things. If someone has a problem and money can solve the problem, they should go to work, get some money, and solve the problem. But there are some problems that money cannot solve. For example, spiritual ignorance, educational ignorance, and even some illnesses cannot be solved with money. Reading is probably a better solution than money in many instances. It is better for an individual to seek the face of God and walk in intellectual integrity than to hook and crook for riches.

"Better is the poor that walketh in his integrity, than he that is perverse in his lips, and is a fool" (Prov. 19:1). This scripture warns Christians about being tempted into sacrificing *integrity* for money. Integrity is intellectual. God deals with us through our intellect. This is precisely why you cannot serve God and money (Matt. 6:24). Ecclesiastes states it in a more profound manner: "Moreover the profit of the earth is for all: the king himself is served by the field. He that loveth silver shall not be satisfied with silver; nor he that loveth abundance with increase: this is also vanity. When goods increase, they are increased that eat them: and what good is there to the owners thereof, saving the beholding of them with their eyes? The sleep of a laboring man is sweet, whether he eats little or much: but the abundance of the rich will not suffer him to sleep" (Eccl. 5:9–12).

This is the epitome of the ungodly greed-factor. Jesus spoke a parable to His disciples: "The ground of a certain rich man brought forth plentifully: and he thought within himself, saying, what shall I do, because I have no room where to bestow all my fruits? And he said. This will I do: I will pull down my barns, and build greater; and there will I bestow all my fruits and goods. And I will say to my soul, Soul, thou hast much goods laid up for many years: take thine ease, eat, drink, and be merry. But God said unto him, Thou fool, this night thy soul shall be required of thee: then whose shall those things be, which thou hast provided? So is he that layeth up treasure for himself, and is not rich toward God" (Luke 12:16–21).

Thus the political fight in American society is over controlling the *evaluation* and *circulation* of the "false god" of this world: money. In fact, the American dollar is the *default currency* of the world community. Jesus declared: "Take no thought for your life, what ye shall eat, or what ye shall drink; nor yet for your body, what ye shall put on. Is not the life more than meat and the body more than raiment? For your Heavenly Father knoweth that ye have need of all these things. Take therefore no thought for the morrow: for the morrow shall take thought for the things of itself. Sufficient unto the day is the evil thereof" (Matt. 6:25–34).

To be sure, *money is a cruel master.* When you love something that cannot love you in return you will be hurt. As Elvis Presley said "don't be cruel" either to self or others because your greatest need is to be loved—and it was love that called you into being. *God is love.* As Christians, God has given us a weapon that we might be able to fight against the wiles of the devil: praise! In American society many states give citizens the right to carry a concealed deadly weapon, **a gun**. Yet God gives every Christian a weapon that they do not have to conceal: PRAISE. *Praise God from whom all blessings flow!* There is victory in

Jesus Christ because God is an awesome, faithful God who never fails to perfect His divine will.

I encourage every reader to have a real-life spiritual encounter with God, coming to know who God is in the pardoning of sins: redemptive salvation. If an individual wants to go to heaven they must know how to climb Jacob's ladder to heaven. The apostle Peter declared that every Christian must become a partaker of the divine nature of God in order to climb Jacob's ladder to heaven. A Christian must:

- Seek first the kingdom of God and all His righteousness.
- Grow in grace and favor with God.
- Add to their faith virtue, knowledge, temperance, patience, godliness, brotherly love, and charity.

Above all, a Christian is an individual who knows who God is and what God demands. The power of God was profoundly expressed in the life and teachings of Jesus Christ, the Righteous One. In the final analysis the New Testament writer Paul said it best: "It is a trustworthy statement, deserving full acceptance, that Christ Jesus came into the world to save sinners, of whom I am the chief" (1 Tim. 1:15). If the chief sinner could experience salvation on the road to Damascus, there is eternal hope for all sinners.

As Americans, we need to be clear about the love of God. As Christians, we need to accept God's laws as the basis for our national life because Christians are defined by their relationship with God. There is a difference between being what you are and being what you would like to be: in the world but not of the world. Be yourself before you are by yourself. Indeed, it is all about family love, because God has family on His mind and family should be on our minds as well. It is in the family context that God's love should be most vividly expressed in our interpersonal relationships.

PRAYER

Praise God from whom all blessings flow. Let the church say amen. Get right, church, let's go home. God, we ask for Your forgiveness for our sins against the church of Jesus Christ. Make us ever mindful of the historical fact that Jesus' blood was shed for us as well as for the church universal. We pray, heavenly Father, that all individuals will follow Your biblical instructions for life before leaving earth so that they might have life more abundantly. For Jesus declared, 'I come that you might have life and have life more abundantly.' Jesus did not come to teach us how to die but rather how to live. As Christians, we are thankful that we serve a God of another chance; Jesus provides us with an avenue for instant forgiveness of our sins. Let the church be the church. Get right, church: the King of Kings is coming. Amen!

Chapter 2

THE DIVINE INSTITUTIONS
OF FAMILY AND CHURCH

> God created man in His own image, in the image of God He
> created him; male and female He created them.
>
> **Genesis 1:27**

LET THE FAMILY BE THE FAMILY

Family is a *divine* institution, not an economic corporation; however all families have economic functions, that is *food, shelter, clothing,* and *transportation* needs. Without a doubt, the family unit is universally accepted as the basis for all societies, yet the economic institution is the dominant institution in societies. The central question is why. Family is about God's love and His spiritual purposes for humanity—a love association of the highest order. Family was designed by God as the school for His *spiritual love*. Indeed, family is the incubator for the nurturing and socialization of children. Thus, family is the basis for personality and character development. Individuals can have family contentment (happiness) if they are willing to pay the cost.

Jesus says: "Whosoever cometh to me, and heareth my sayings, and doeth them, I will shew you to whom he is like: he is like a man which built a house, and digged deep, and laid a foundation on a rock: and when the flood arose, the stream beat vehemently upon that house, and could not shake it: for it was founded upon a rock. But he that heareth, and doeth not, is like a man that without a foundation built an house upon the earth; against which the stream did beat vehemently, and immediately it fell; and the ruin of that house was great" (Luke 6:47–49). A family unit must be built upon a foundation of *godly love* to withstand the wiles of the devil. Families might from time to time run out of money but they should never run out of love, because love is infinite.

One never really gets something for nothing; life is not that simple. For after all nothing from nothing leaves nothing. This is why Jesus always urged anticipating the cost. Again, family must be based upon *unconditional love*. Unfortunately, the competition for material goodies has become so fierce that it forces members of a family to function as individualists rather than as a spiritual love association. To be sure, divorce rate, family size, abortion, nursing/retirement homes, and above all child neglect and abuse are all directly related to the sometimes vulgar materialistic nature of our economic system and the values that undergird our collective mentality. Any economic system that *glorifies* materialism as a way of life destroys the basis of society (family moral order)—that is the valuation of the sanctity of life and family.

THE QUALITIES OF A SPIRITUAL FAMILY

A spiritual family must be based on "friendship," which combines temperamental compatibility, sympathetic understanding, mutual confidence, and high moral ideals. A spiritual family begins at the marriage altar. A spiritual family:

- assumes *equality* of responsibility and democracy in reaching family decisions, not arbitrariness.
- stresses the significance of spiritual living for the development of human personality, intellectual integrity, and character development.
- recognizes that personal happiness is to be achieved and secured through family relationships.
- stresses the principle of loving/sacrificing/giving rather than receiving and taking.

A spiritual family has the Spirit of God at the center of family life: at the marriage altar, when the new home is built, when the baby comes, and above all when hard times come.

The church house is *God's house* and Jesus is the foundation, and it is in the church house where the meaning of family life ought to be illuminated. Therefore making family life creatively religious is a *collective responsibility*.

THE ROLE OF A SPIRITUAL MOTHER

A spiritual mother is the cement that holds a family together. God is at the center of a spiritual family, and a spiritual mother's love is the foundation. It is virtually impossible to drive a loving spiritual mother away from her collective responsibility to her family. A spiritually loving mother doesn't just smooth things over but mends them with love.

Spiritual mothers have an abiding faith in the *faithfulness of God*, because undefiled religion is the crown of womanhood. Without a doubt, God's love is limitless, but I have never seen an individual that was saved from "self" who did not have a loving spiritual mother.

Spiritual mothers are faithful to themselves first of all by being faithful to God. For after all, who among us have not laid our burdens, sins, sorrows, heartaches, and weaknesses on the shrine of mother's love? Thanks be to God for spiritual mothers, because it is ungodly that many spiritual mothers have to perform double duty because many *carnal-minded fathers* are MIA (missing in action). "For if any provide not for his own, and especially for those of his own house, he hath denied the faith, and is worse than an infidel" (1 Tim. 5:8). MIA fathers are neither good nor godly.

A GODLY MAN IS A GOOD MAN

> Blessed is the man that walketh not in the counsel of the ungodly, nor standeth in the way of sinners, nor sitteth in the seat of the scornful. But his delight is in the law of the Lord; and in his law doth he meditate day and night. And he shall be like a tree planted by the rivers of water, that bringeth forth his fruit in his season; his leaf also shall not wither; and whatsoever he doeth shall prosper. The ungodly are not so: but are like chaff which the wind driveth away. Therefore the ungodly shall not stand in the judgment, nor sinners in the congregation of the righteous. For the Lord knoweth the way of the righteous: but the way of the ungodly shall perish.
>
> **Psalm 1:1–6**

A godly man understands God's principles, and of course God's principles are not popular. A godly man knows that he is required to have the character of God, exemplified in the life of Jesus. "The steps of a good man are ordered by the Lord: and he delighteth in his way. Though He fall, he shall not be utterly cast down: for the Lord upholdeth him with his hand. I have been young, and now am old, yet I have not seen the righteous forsaken, nor his seed begging bread" (Psalms 37: 23–25).

A godly man is a worthy teacher/trainer, willing not only to live by every word that proceeds from God's mouth, but also by every word that comes out of his own mouth. But most of all a godly man understands God's plan for heaven on earth. "What is man, that thou shouldest magnify him? And that thou shouldest set thine heart upon him? And that thou shouldest visit him every morning, and try him every moment?" (Job 7:17–18). Hebrews 2:6 raises the question in this manner: "What is man, that thou art mindful of him? Or the son of man, that thou visitest him?"

God's plan for man is that he simply be a witness for the truth: *God.* A godly man understands the purpose(s) of God. For without a doubt, the purpose of God is that man should glorify Him. When a man abides in God's principles, executes God's plan, and honors God's purpose there is salvation for the soul. Men ought to let the light of their lives so shine that others might see their good works in their homes, churches, neighborhoods, and society in general. The works of a good man should glorify God, not glorify self. Above all, a godly man understands the importance of positive *scriptural/spiritual self-talk.*

"For what is a man profited, if he shall gain the whole world, and lose his own soul? Or what shall a man give in exchange for his soul?" (Matt. 16:26). Indeed, *soul* is an intangible; it cannot be bought and sold, only given away. "Take heed, and beware of covetousness: for a man's life consisteth not in the abundance of the things he possesseth" (Luke 12:15). Without a doubt, money is a cruel master because the love of money is the root of all evil.

A godly man understands family unity-cooperation, and he wants *cooperation* (help-meet) from a woman, and of course a woman wants *love* from a man. Therefore a man is God's glory, and we know that God is love. A woman is man's glory, and a woman's glory is her hair.

> For a man indeed ought not to cover his head, forasmuch as he is the image and glory of God: but a woman is the glory of a man. For the man is not of the woman: but the woman of the man. Neither was the man created for the woman, but the woman for the man. For this cause ought the woman to have power on her head because of the angels. Nevertheless neither is the man without the woman, neither the woman without the man, in the Lord. For as the woman is of the man, even so is the man also of the woman; but all things are of God. Doth not even nature itself teach you, that, if a man has long hair, it is a shame unto him? But if a woman has long hair, it is glory to her: for her hair is given her for a covering.
>
> 1 Corinthians 11:7–15

A woman's glory is her hair (*vanity*). Since a man is *God's glory*, and therefore he must be like God, he has a more difficult task because he has no *visual pattern to follow; except the spiritual life of Jesus Christ as recorded in Holy Scriptures.* Hence, a man must see his pattern (God) with the *eyes of his mind.* On the other hand, a woman can do anything a man can do simply because she has a *visual-physical pattern*—the principle of "monkey see monkey do." Imitation is not always flattery; sometimes it's suicide. Of course, the best principle is to be what you are in God. Imitate God. Therefore, the weaker vessel can be either male or female. The Christian church needs to develop strategies for *holy* matrimony and spiritual moral family integration, not same-sex marriage.

For a *real man* love is simply spiritual protection and provision, because God is divine protection and provision. "But my God shall supply all your need according to his riches in glory by Christ Jesus" (Phil. 4:19). MIA fathers, I encourage you with this thought: "If ye continue in my word, then are ye my disciples indeed: and ye shall know the truth, and the truth shall make you free" (John 8:31–32). A real man not only morally leads his family and provides for their physical needs, he leaves a lasting heritage. "A good man leaves an inheritance to his children's children, but the wealth of the sinner is stored up for the righteous" (Prov. 13:22). This is precisely why the role of the mother in teaching love is so important in a family structure. "And he will turn the hearts of the fathers to the children, and the hearts of the children to their fathers, lest I come and strike the earth with a curse" (Mal. 4:6). This is why mothers should teach children to love their fathers, so that they might love and respect their mothers as well as others.

In short, God designed family to help us become what He wants us to be in Him, not for ourselves but for each other. Be what you are, not for selfish reasons, but in order that God might be glorified. To be what you are is to be in *submission* to the will of God, not seek to follow your own way, since there is no genuine "own way." "Enter ye in at the strait gate: for wide is the gate, and broad is the way, that leadeth to destruction, and many there be which go in thereat. Because strait is the gate, and narrow is the way, which leadeth unto life, and few there be that find it" (Matt. 7:13–14). The only true way is God's way.

Without a doubt, we are what we are through what God did in and through His Son Jesus Christ. God humbled Himself in the form of a man (Jesus) and suffered for our sins in order that we might be *saved* from the world's slow stain. "Be ye therefore followers of God, as dear children; and walk in love as Christ also hath loved us, and hath given himself for us an offering and a sacrifice to God for a sweet-smelling savor" (Eph. 5:1–2). As Christians we are commanded to bear one another's burdens, which in turn is the fulfillment of the holiness of the *law of Christ*. "Bear ye one another's burdens, and so fulfill the law of Christ. For if any man thinks himself to be something, when he is nothing, he deceiveth himself" (Gal. 6:2–3).

God ordained the family unit as a system of spiritual cooperation. "Let the husband render under the wife due benevolence: and likewise also the wife unto the husband. The wife hath not power of her own body, but the husband: and likewise also the husband hath not power of his own body, but the wife. Defraud ye not one the other, except it be with consent for a time, that ye may give yourselves to fasting and prayer; and come together again, that Satan tempt you not for your incontinency" (1 Cor. 7:3–5).

Cooperation is about individuals learning how to restrain themselves to achieve a greater purpose. *Marriage, to God, is about godly human sexuality and procreation*. When a woman gives herself to a man—that is allows him to undercover her *nakedness*, and they engage in *sexuality* in the sight of God—that act constitutes marriage. Godly marriage is about "submitting you one to another in fear of God. Wives, submit yourselves unto your own husbands, as unto the Lord. For the husband is the head of the wife, even as Christ is the head of the church: and he is the savior of the body. Therefore, as the church is subject unto Christ, so let the wives be to their own husbands in everything. Husbands love your wives, even as Christ also loved the church, and gave himself for it; that he might sanctify and cleanse it with the washing of the word, that he might present it to himself a glorious church, not having a spot or wrinkle, or any such thing; but that it should be holy and without blemish" (Eph. 5:21–27).

Unfortunately, too many men do not understand this simple yet profound spiritual truth. Men, rule over your wives and children with love, not dictatorial arbitrariness. But, more importantly, understand that when you *uncover sexually a woman's nakedness* in the sight of

God you are responsible for her well-being. Now we understand why *illegitimate parents, not illegitimate children,* represent a real moral problem for American society. Sexuality and money should not be used as spiritual weapons of warfare in marriage and family relations. In other words, women use sexuality to subdue men and men use money to subdue women instead of both using love to strengthen each other. Indeed it is immoral for a husband to rape his wife. Spiritual family unity is the godly basis for lasting societal moral order, not civilian police departments. Indeed, family spiritual unity must be the basis for societal moral order.

Submission is about women and men cooperating with each other out of godly love for each other and respect for God the Father. Men and women ought to submit one to the other out of fear of God. "Even as Sara obeyed Abraham, calling him Lord: whose daughters ye are, as long as ye do well, and are not afraid with any amazement. Likewise, ye husbands dwell with them according to knowledge, giving honor unto the wife, as unto the weaker vessel, and as being heirs together of the grace of life; that your prayers be not hindered. Finally, *be ye* all of one mind, having compassion one of another, love as brethren, be pitiful, be courteous: not rendering evil for evil, or railing for railing: but contrariwise blessing; knowing that ye are thereunto called, that ye should inherit a blessing" (1 Pet. 3:6–9).

Civilian police departments are necessary to maintain *superficial moral order* based upon external physical authority: guns and clubs. It is not cost-effective for society to employ a police officer for every individual. Therefore, *real moral order* comes from internal *spiritually* directed self-restraint and self-control. The family unit is the *basic training unit for establishing moral order,* the foundation for a righteous society. Indeed children imitate what they see. If children witness conflict and strife within the family context they take that same mental attitude to school and society in general. Removing the symbol of *sacredness-prayer* from schools obviously did not help to maintain moral stability in schools or society in general. For after all, symbols motivate human behavior.

However, this book is not about public school politics per se but about righteousness, good understanding, and above all what makes for a moral society. "Righteousness exalteth a nation: but sin is a reproach to any people" (Prov. 14:34). In my opinion it is better to have a righteous society and an immoral individual than an immoral society and a righteous individual. Group influence tends to be more powerful than individual persuasion.

Children must be nurtured in environments where they observe their parents loving and cooperating with each other and resolving values conflicts non-violently. Unfortunately, too many parents are living unconscious lives before their children, not thinking about how their attitudes and behavior affect the attitudes and behavior of their children. For after all, human conflict is most definitely about values conflict. Values are simply about priorities. Priorities are about *importance ordering*. Therefore, for a child to be conceived and born into this world, cooperation between a man and a woman should prevail, not conflict. Spiritual unity must exist between a husband and a wife in order to have *family unity*. When children grow up learning to resolve conflict non-violently within the family context, they are more likely to seek a non-violent resolution to conflict in school environments and society in general. Bullying in schools probably would not exist.

This is precisely why God ordained family as a *system of spiritual cooperation*. That is husbands and wives spiritually cooperating with each other, children cooperating with parents, and siblings cooperating with each other. Truly, families that *pray* together stay together, because prayer is *internal self-introspection*. Having a little spiritual conversation (*talk*) with Jesus and one's self is what prayer is all about. Jesus is sitting at the right hand of God the Father making intercession on our behalf. When you pray you go into the closet of your own mind (being) and bring the "I" that is the ego (*selfishness/self-centeredness*) in you under submission to the "me" in you. The *me* is the spiritual part of your being that will call out "Lord, have mercy upon me a sinner and a wretch undone." Joshua 24:14–15 states it plainly: "Now therefore fear the Lord, and serve him in sincerity and in truth: and put away the gods which your fathers served on the other side of the flood, and in Egypt; and serve ye the Lord. And if it seems evil unto you to serve the Lord, choose you this day whom ye will serve; whether the gods which your fathers served that was on the other side of the flood, or the gods of the Amorites, in whose land you dwell: but as for me and my house, we will serve the Lord."

Again, for parents to bring their children under prayerful parental subordination they must see and experience love and spiritual cooperation within the family context. This is the best form of discipline that children could ever experience, spiritually as well as socially. "Children, obey your parents in the Lord: for this is right. Honor your father and mother; which is the first commandment with promise; that it may be well with thee, and thou may live long on the earth. And, ye fathers, provoke not your children to wrath: but bring them up in the nurture and admonition of the Lord" (Eph. 6:1–4).

Men are primarily responsible for maintaining sacredness both within the family context and in God's creation. "Thou shalt fear the Lord thy God, and serve him, and shalt swear by his name. Ye shall not go after other gods, of the gods of the people round about you; for the Lord thy God is a jealous God among you lest the anger of the Lord thy God be kindled against thee, and destroy thee off the face of the earth" (Deut. 6:13).

"Adam, where art thou?" This question is universal in nature and also transcends time. Even in twenty-first-century America the question is still relevant because God says: "Therefore shall a man leave his father and his mother, and shall cleave unto his wife: and they shall be one flesh. And they were both naked, the man and his wife, and were not ashamed" (Gen. 2:24–25). Of course, the answer to the question "Where art thou?" is this: *too many fathers are not at home! Too many mothers are frustrated because they are raising children alone. Too many fatherless children are misbehaving out of unbridled rage!* As a result, American society has become a ball of immoral confusion.

The Bible warns us about the consequences of forgetting God, because in times of plenty it is easy to think that our prosperity is the result of our own ingenuity, hard work, and self-sacrifice. It is God who blesses us with abundance, and it is God who wants us to manage it for His kingdom building.

> Beware that you forget not the Lord thy God, in not keeping his commandments, and his judgments, and his statutes, which I command thee this day: Lest when thou hast eaten and art full, and hast built goodly houses, and dwelt therein; and when thy herds and thy flocks multiply, and thy silver and thy gold is multiplied, and all thou hast is multiplied; then thine heart be lifted up, and thou forget the Lord thy God, which brought thee forth out of the land of Egypt, from the house of bondage.... And thou say in thine heart my power and the might of mine hand hath gotten me this wealth. But thou shalt remember the Lord thy God: for it is he that giveth thee power to get wealth that he may establish his covenant which he swore unto thou fathers, as it is this day. And it shall be, if thou do at all forget the Lord thy God, and walk after other gods, and serve them, and worship them, I testify against you this day that ye shall surely perish. As the nations which the Lord destroyeth before your face, so shall ye perish; because ye would not be obedient unto the voice of the Lord your God.
>
> Deuteronomy 8:11–20

Pride goes before a fall. We live in an imperfect world because of sin. Our boasting is in the Lord, but we should take pride in spiritual family unity, giving God the glory. Freedom is not acquired through irresponsible conduct, and of course *sin* does not exist because of lack of knowledge. Too many fathers have abandoned their families, especially their children, and are in the world attempting to acquire freedom by being irresponsible. Freedom is not free. Absentee fathers have provoked their children into *unbridled wrath*, and in so doing they have already lost their souls in this world prior to physical death. *Salvation indeed comes through the generations.*

For example, the book of Matthew begins with the genealogy of Jesus Christ, the Righteous One. Jesus came through forty-two generations of individuals who called upon the Lord, did God's will, and lived righteously before God.

Without a doubt, the unbridled wrath in today's children has produced a generation with *bad attitudes*, and bad attitudes place bricks on prison walls; in other words, in American society we are now building more prisons to *warehouse* children than first-class schools to educate children. This social fact in and of itself is a sad commentary on the spiritual condition of American society. It does not get better, only worse, because of the total deterioration of both nuclear as well as extended family structures.

The cornerstone of American *godly* cultural values is mass universal education. The founding fathers, especially George Washington, desired an American citizenry that could read and write, especially read the Bible. "Having thus imparted to you my sentiments as they have been awakened by the occasion that brings us together, I shall take my present leave; but not without resorting once more to the benign Parent of the human race in humble supplication that, since He has been pleased to favor the American people with opportunities for deliberating in perfect tranquility, and dispositions for deciding with unparalleled unanimity on a form of government for the security of their union and the advancement of their happiness, so His divine blessing may be equally conspicuous in the enlarged views, the temperate consultations and the wise measures on which the success of this government must depend" (George Washington).

Therefore, we must spiritually reorient American society to the realization that God is "A father of the fatherless, a defender of widows, is God in His holy habitation" (Ps. 68:5). "Leave your fatherless children, I will preserve them alive; and let your widows trust in me" (Jer. 49:11). Only the *New Testament church* is living by the unadulterated Word of God: doing benevolence and loving and serving. Jesus says: "A new commandment I give to you, that ye love one another; as I have loved you, that ye also love one another. By this shall all men know that ye are my disciples, if ye have love one to another" (John 13:34–35).

The church of Jesus Christ teaches godly principles in order that Christian believers are equipped to teach and be examples of the Word of God to others. "These things teach and exhort. If any man teach otherwise, and consent not to the wholesome words, even the words of our Lord Jesus Christ, and to the doctrine which is according to godliness; he is proud, knowing nothing, but doting about questions and strifes of words, whereof cometh envy, strife, railings, evil surmisings, perverse disputings of men of corrupt minds, and destitute of the truth, supposing that gain is godliness: from such withdraw thyself. But godliness with contentment is great gain" (1 Tim. 6: 2–6).

Great living or low-life living costs individuals something. Indeed the price tag on a Christian home is high. "For which of you, intending to build a tower, sitteth down first, and counteth the cost, whether he have sufficient to finish it. Lest haply, after he hath laid the foundation, and is not able to finish it, all that behold it begin to mock him, saying, this man began to build, and was not able to finish" (Luke 14:28).

Family is the basis for individuals fulfilling God's fourfold positional foundation for human existence:

Family is the basis for human beings becoming *fruitful, multiplying, replenishing the earth, and subduing it.* In order for family life to become creatively more religious, individuals must learn how to put more affection in their love. In so doing, we fulfill the law of Christ by bearing one another's burdens. In other words, evaluate each other more wisely by overlooking poor points and stressing the good ones. This makes for a positive attitude toward life, because it is Godly principles that strengthens families.

CHARACTERISTICS OF A GODLY FAMILY

- Built on a love that develops through association before marriage
- Based upon friendship which combines temperamental compatibility
- Assumes equality of the sexes and democracy in decision-making
- Stresses the significance of family for the development of healthy personality structures
- Recognizes personal happiness as an objective to be secured through marriage and family
- Allows individuals to achieve family happiness if they are willing to count the cost and pay the price tag

PRAYER

Heavenly Father, we pray that every family chooses life and Your blessings, not Your curses. Above all, that every family learn to love You as well as each other, obey Your Word, walk in Your precepts, and be faithful to You by not creating spiritual prisons for self and others. Let the church be the church. Get right, church. The King of Kings is coming. Amen!

Chapter 3

THE CHURCH OF
JESUS CHRIST

And I say unto thee, that thou art Peter, and upon this rock
I will build my church; and the gates of hell shall not prevail
against it.

Matthew 16:18

To reiterate, the Garden of Eden was the church. God spiritually
met in fellowship and partnership with Adam and Eve there. Both
their spiritual and physical needs could be fulfilled in the Garden of
Eden. In the twenty-first-century Christian church the same format
should exist.

Without a doubt, the first Christian church was Jesus and the
twelve disciples. On the one hand, the Christian church is *God's spiritual
business*, not a manmade *creation*, and the very gates of hell shall not

prevail against it. On the other hand, *social democracy* is humanity seeking to work out ethical/moral resource allocation in society. A Christian's moral duty is to be in the world but not of the world, simply because the devil is the *prince* of this world. If you are a disciple of the prince of the world then you are no longer a child of the Father in heaven who created the world; you are of your father, the prince of the world, who is the devil (John 8:44). We can deduce from this historical fact that it takes godly men to build strong spiritual churches as well as strong communities.

Jesus' life was an example to the disciples as well as to twenty-first-century Christians on *how to do, what to do, when to do, and above all what not to do to obtain eternal life.* "Let not your heart be troubled: ye believe in God, believe also in me. In my Father's house are many mansions: if it were not so, I would have told you. I go to prepare a place for you. And if I go and prepare a place for you, I will come again, and receive you unto myself; that where I am, there ye may be also" (John 14:1–3). No individual can be saved in Pastor Joe Moe Blow's church or any other person's so-called church: salvation is only associated with the *church from Christ* (Matt. 16:18). Even Jesus' encounter with the Samaritan woman at the well illustrates this point (John 4:5–29). For after all, Jesus told the woman not to go back to the Temple without the *covering* of her husband, since she'd had five husbands and the man she was currently with was not her husband.

Without a doubt, Jesus recruited and trained converted men, *men who had repented of their sins* to become leaders in the church because of their leadership qualifications. No test, no testimony. The disciples had been tested, and each had a powerful testimony about the goodness of God as exemplified by the teachings of Jesus as well as how Jesus lived. Hence, institutional Christianity needs to develop strategies for becoming a *prophetic religion* (Christ-centered Christianity); rather than a pathetic carbon-copy of secular society, which includes strategies for thinking spiritually and acting ethically politically. The issue is Christ-centered Christianity versus Culture Christianity.

Therefore, the divine order of the church is: (1) God the Father, (2) God the Son, (3) God the Holy Spirit/Truth, and (4) Christian believers: men/women/children. The Bible is the instructional guide. This divine order is the basis for individual as well as family spiritual growth and development. For after all, family is what the church is all about, and God always has family on His mind. As head of the church Jesus ordered His living by *God's Word and God's will.* "Trust in the Lord with all your heart; and lean not unto thine own understanding. In all thy ways acknowledge Him, and He will direct your paths" (Prov. 3:5).

Double-minded pastors ought to be concerned about the greater condemnation for false teachings: "My brethren, be not many masters, knowing that we shall receive the greater condemnation" (James 3:1). The book of 1 Peter profoundly expresses it in this manner: "Neither as being lords over God's heritage, but being examples to the flock" (1 Pet. 5:3). Greater condemnation simply means *stricter* judgment—that is you have knowingly led individuals to hell for the *love of money.*

The *love of money* is the root of all kinds of evil because money is indeed a very cruel master, simply because money has no intellect. If you are seeking first the kingdom of God and His righteousness, then "all these things" are added unto you. But money is the answer only to the things of this world. "A feast is made for laughter, and wine maketh merry: but money answereth all things" (Eccl. 10:19). Why? Because the business people of this world want money for their things—their *stuff.* The question is, are they spiritually righteous? Seeking first the kingdom of God? It's not about political ideology but spiritual-ology. Some might ask why the emphasis on money. The answer is simply that more often than not in Christian churches the emphasis is on the collection plate. Therefore, rather than the prophetic emphasis being on love and service, it is on money. Of course, money itself is value neutral but the human greed factor causes money to have a corrupting influence on individuals, institutions, and society in general.

The prophet Malachi records God as saying, "Will a man rob God? Yet ye have robbed me. But ye say wherein have we robbed thee? In tithes and offerings. Ye are cursed with a curse; for ye have robbed me, even this whole nation. Bring ye all the tithes into the storehouse, that there may be meat in mine house, and prove me now herewith, saith the Lord of Hosts, if I will not open you the windows of heaven, and pour you out a blessing, that there shall not be room enough to receive it" (Mal. 3:8–10).

God is the basis for morality, and when religious leaders become double-minded because of the love of money, political leaders inevitably become more confused and greedy and will sell out voters—the universal common good for the largest corporate brown bag. In some instances, politicians and pastors have formed an ungodly alliance. Indeed this ungodly alliance has at times helped to fuel the moral denigration of American society. To restate, the church must always think spiritually in order to be the church, but act in political ways without embracing partisan politics.

What is the church? The church belongs to Jesus Christ simply because the church is founded upon the *immaculate-conception birth*, *life, death, resurrection,* and *ascension of Jesus* (1 Cor. 15:1–4). "Moreover, brethren, I declare unto you the gospel which I preached unto you, which also ye have received, and wherein ye stand: by which also ye are saved, if ye keep in memory what I preached unto you, unless ye believed in vain. For I delivered unto you first of all that which I also received, how Christ died for our sins according to the scriptures, and that he was buried, and that he rose again the third day according to the scriptures." Christian friends, this is the *gospel of Good News.* Jesus is the Word of God made flesh. "In the beginning was the Word, and the Word was with God, and the Word was God. The same was in the beginning with God. All things were made by Him, and without him was not anything made that was made. In him was life; and the life was the light of men" (John 1:1–5).

God sent a man named John to be a voice crying in the wilderness: "repent for the kingdom of God is at hand." Wilderness simply means ignorant people: people who do not know God. Or better still, individuals who are willing to lose what they have, seeking to obtain what they do not need. John became known as John the Baptist because of the sacrament of baptism (John 1:19–34).

Jesus went to John and asked him to baptize Him. Initially, John refused to baptize Jesus, whom he referred to as the Lamb of God that takes away the sins of the world. John finally consented to baptize Jesus in the Jordan River, and for the second time in recorded biblical history God speaks directly from heaven when the Spirit in the form of a dove descends from heaven and says, "This is my beloved Son in whom I am well pleased." Basically, the Christian church only has two sacraments, baptism and the Lord's Supper.

The church is the pillar and foundation of ultimate societal *truth* and is therefore the basis for moral order and civility in society. When the church ceases to function in this spiritual role it ceases to be the church of Jesus Christ. "But if I tarry long, thou mayest know how thou oughtest behave thyself in the house of God, which is the church of the living God, the pillar and ground of the truth" (1 Tim. 3:15).

Who is the church? The church is the called-out body of believers. "Ye are the light of the world. A city set on a hill cannot be hid. Neither do men light a candle, and put it under a bushel, but on a candle stick; and it giveth light unto all that are in the house. Let your light so shine before men, that they may see your good works, and glorify your Father which is in heaven" (Matt. 5:16–17). The twenty-first-century church has been hijacked by double-minded pastors, and God is not pleased.

Daniel spoke prophetically concerning the trials and tribulations of the church during the times of the Herodian kings: "And in the days of these kings shall the God of heaven set up a kingdom, which shall never be destroyed: and the kingdom shall not be let to other people, but it shall break in pieces and consume all these kingdoms, and it shall stand for ever" (Dan. 2:44). God said, "Do My will." Jesus said, "Do the will of My Father that sent Me." Jesus was speaking of the Trinitarian nature of the Godhead: God the Father, God the Son, and God the Holy Spirit (Truth/Action).

American society is losing generation after generation to immorality, unrighteousness, and relativism. Fewer of America's children go to church than ever before, and likewise fewer are raised in two-parent households or trained in the way of the Lord. Every generation is becoming "wiser" and more unrighteous than the previous generation. We are living in an age in which we have become fearful of our own children. Truly successful children are children that have been trained in the ways of the Lord, not the ways of the world.

When I was growing up there were two individuals you did not want your parents insisting that you must talk to: the pastor and the principal. These professionals were the most highly respected individuals in the community because they understood the dos and don'ts of moral Christian leadership (Matthew 10). "And that from a child thou hast known the holy scriptures, which are able to make thee wise unto salvation through faith which is in Christ Jesus" (2 Tim. 3:15–16).

WHAT'S WRONG WITH THE CHURCH?

Jesus' Great Commission to the church is not about individualistic wealth creation but saving souls. "All power is given unto me in heaven and earth. Go ye therefore, and teach all nations, baptizing them in the name of the Father, and of the Son, and of the Holy Ghost: Teaching them to observe all things whatsoever I have commanded you: and, lo, I am with you always, even unto the end of the world. Amen" (Matt. 28:18–20).

In recent months, in metropolitan Houston, several prominent pastoral leaders have been criminally convicted and given prison time for stealing hundreds of thousands of dollars from the local congregations they were blessed and *privileged* to pastor. These salacious stories have made shameful news headlines. On the one hand, the devil desires to shame the church of Jesus Christ so that individuals might stop going to church. Of course, this is exactly why an individual should have church (*individual/family consecration*) before they go to church houses. On the other hand, God desires that the church *first exist in individual conscience* and therefore be *consecrated creatively in family life.* "For we are laborers together with God: ye are God's husbandry, ye are God's building" (1 Cor. 3:9). God's church begins in the heart of individual conscience— sacredness toward heavenly things. "Know ye not that ye are the temple of God, and that the spirit of God dwelleth in you?" (1 Cor. 3:16).

Too many double-minded pastoral leaders desire to operate churches as *economic business enterprises* rather than as God's spiritual business: soul saving. As a result, these double-minded pastors desire accountability to an "invisible God," not a real God that works in and through people to perfect His will. Jesus declared,

> For the Son of Man is come to save that which was lost. How think ye? If a man have an hundred sheep, and one of them be gone astray, doth he not leave the ninety nine, and goeth into the mountains, and seeketh that which is gone astray? And if so be that he find it, verily I say unto you, he rejoiceth more of that sheep, than of the ninety and nine which went not astray. Even so it is not the will of your Father, which is in heaven, that one of these little ones should perish. Moreover if thy brother should trespass against thee, go and tell him his fault between

thee and him alone: if he shall hear thee, thou hast gained thy brother. But if he will not hear thee, then take with thee one or two more, that in the mouth of two or three every word may be established. And if he neglects to hear them, tell it unto the church: but if he neglects to hear the church, let him be unto thee as a heathen man and a publican. Verily I say unto you, whatsoever ye shall bind on earth shall be bound in heaven: and whatsoever ye shall loose on earth shall be loosed in heaven. Again, I say unto you, that if two of you shall agree on earth as touching anything that they shall ask, it shall be done for them of my Father which is in heaven. For where two or three are gathered together in my name, there am I in the midst of them.

Matthew 18:11–20

My Christian friends, this is what church life is all about: individuals gathering in the name of Jesus and agreeing in one accord in the name of Jesus. The *church universal*—Jesus' church—is not about meeting the *vanity needs* of self-serving, unaccountable, double-minded pastors who desire that parishioners "do as I say, not as I do." Therefore, lest we forget:

To the general assembly and the church of the first born, which was written in heaven, and to God the judge of all, and to the spirits of just men made perfect, and to Jesus the mediator of the new covenant, and to the blood of sprinkling, that speaketh better things than that of Abel. See that ye refuse not him that speaketh. For if they escaped not who refused him that spake on earth, much more shall not we escape, if we turn away from him that speaketh from heaven: whose voice then shook the earth: but now he hath promised, saying, Yet once more I shake not only the earth, but also heaven. And this word, yet once

more signifieth the removing of those things that are shaken,
as of things that are made, that those things which cannot be
shaken remain. Wherefore we are receiving a kingdom which
cannot be moved, let us have grace, whereby we may serve
God acceptably with reverence and godly fear: For our God is
a consuming fire.

Hebrews 12:23–29

Judgment is at hand for the twenty-first-century church.

The devil attacked the church in the first century just as he is
attacking the church in the twenty-first century. Even in Old Testament
times the devil sought to disrupt God's soul-salvation plan. Isaiah
declared: "His watchmen are blind: they are all ignorant, they are dumb
dogs, they cannot bark; sleeping, lying down, and loving to slumber.
Yea they are greedy dogs which can never have enough, and they are
shepherds that cannot understand: they all look to their own way, every
one for his gain, for his quarter. Come ye, say they, I will fetch wine, and
we will fill ourselves with strong drink; and tomorrow shall be as this day
and much more abundant" (Isa. 56:10–12).

While there are too many double-minded pastoral leaders in
America's pulpits who will not speak truth to power, there are also too
many *bench-warming* Christians who will not hold religious leadership
accountable. Indeed this combination is a recipe for *culture Christianity*
rather than authentic Christianity: the church of Jesus Christ. In fact,
we have Christianity from the pulpit rather than from the Bible, because
the Bible's way is God's way.

As the holy Trinity, God the Father brought order to the world
(universe) through love, God the Son brought redemption to the world
through love and service, and the Holy Spirit (the Comforter) brings
God's truth to the world through comforting. Of course, the Bible is the
standard bearer of the "three in one."

In the worldly trinity, *theology* is human interpretation of the Bible oriented toward humans seeking to make sense of the meaning of life. Sometimes theology becomes mankind's rationalization to justify human frailties and shortcomings. But, more importantly, theology is humankind's understanding of the *vertical* relationship between the individual and God.

Sociology is humankind's understanding of the *horizontal* relationship between individuals—that is how we learn to live with each other without killing one another when values-conflict arises between individuals and nations.

Psychology is a study of the workings of the mind as it relates to human interaction both individual and as a group. Psychology is an understanding of the *life of the mind*, or how individuals learn to live with "self." There is an old adage: "Be yourself before you are by yourself." Integrity oriented individuals do not deal in superficiality or enjoy associating with phony-baloney individuals. To thy own self be true and therefore you cannot be false to others. Of course, the basis for sociology and psychology is theology because these disciplines have their origin in theological concepts, with interpretations in many different books. In conclusion of the matter, the three disciplines in the world trinity are simply representations of Jesus' two great commandments: "Love God with all your heart, soul, and might. Love your neighbor as you love yourself, and do unto others as you would have them do to you."

Theology is housed in these scriptures: "Nevertheless the foundation of God standeth sure, having this seal; the Lord knoweth them that are his. And, let everyone that nameth the name of Christ depart from iniquity" (2 Tim. 2:19). And, "Therefore being justified by faith, we have peace with God through our Lord Jesus Christ" (Rom. 5:1).

Sociology is housed in these scriptures: "And brought them out, and said, Sirs, what must I do to be saved? And they said, Believe on the Lord

Jesus Christ, and thou shalt be saved, and thy house" (Acts 16:30–31). Joshua said to the people of Israel: "But as for me and my house, we will serve the Lord" (Josh. 24:15).

Psychology is housed in these scriptures: "Let this mind be in you, which was also in Christ Jesus" (Phil. 2:5). And, "And the peace of God, which passeth all understanding, shall keep your hearts and minds through Christ Jesus" (Phil. 4:7). When individuals have the mind of Christ they are *content* with whatever state they find themselves in because they are willing to work for what they need and delay gratification of what they think they want.

The problem is the world trinity, not the holy Trinity, simply because *the world trinity seeks to bastardize the holy Trinity.* The consequence of this ungodly effort is monumental confusion that seeks to justify moral-corruption. "For God is not the author of confusion, but of peace, as in all churches of the saints" (1 Cor. 14:33). Therefore, every individual should be mindful of an eternal fact of life: "For the wages of sin is death; but the gift of God is eternal life through Jesus Christ our Lord" (Rom. 6:23). *Corruption is sin and sin is corruption.* God says: "Let all things be done decently and in order" (1 Cor. 14:40). Fellow Americans, right is right and wrong is wrong, yet there is a right way to do wrong according to the world. Of course, the Bible declares that there is a way that seems right to a man, but the end thereof is death. The "right way to do wrong" is an integration of the world trinity into the holy Trinity with some biblical truth, which in turn is sin to the *nth* degree.

In the book of Revelation, the apostle John addresses the seven churches in Asia as these churches were functioning outside the divine order Jesus established for His church. Six of these churches got comfortable and turned inward to serve the ego interests of Christian leaders, just as the church in the twenty-first century has done. God said to the seven churches of Asia:

I know thy works, and thy labor, and thy patience, and how thou canst not bear them that are evil: and thou hast tried them that say they are apostles, and are not, and have found them liars: and hast patience. And my name sake hast labored, and hast not fainted. Nevertheless I have somewhat against thee, because thou hast left thy first love. Remember therefore from whence thou art fallen, and repent, and do the first works; or else I will come unto thee quickly, and will remove thy candlestick out of this place, except thou repent. But this thou hast, that thou hatest the deeds of the Nicolaitans, which I also hate. He that hath an ear, let him hear what the Spirit saith unto the churches; to him that over cometh will I give to eat of the tree of life, which is in the midst of the paradise of God.

Revelation 2:2–7

Christian leaders can hide their *motives and actions* from people, but not from God, because God says *I know your works*. The only one of the seven churches of Asia that was functioning according to God's principles was the church at Philadelphia. There was more corruption in these six churches than in the world, and because of this corruption God allowed Christians to be placed in the lion's den. Of course, some Christians were God-fearing and willingly went into the lion's den. In the first century there were a few Daniels.

Where are the Daniels of the twenty-first century? The answer is: *I don't know*. It's like trying to find a needle in a haystack. Name the sin and the church can produce the exhibit. Unfortunately, we have too many *motivational* speakers rather than *salvation teachers/preachers of the gospel of Good News*. "Study to shew thyself approved of God, a workman that needeth not be ashamed, rightly dividing the word of truth. But shun profane and vain babbling: for they will increase unto more ungodliness" (2 Tim. 2:15–16).

No more rapping, it's time for mapping. As the infamous James Brown so eloquently stated, "Talking loud and saying nothing." In short, stop *whooping* and teach *God's Word* to God's people. We have too few churches that consistently deal with the Great Commission. "All power is given unto me in heaven and in earth. Go ye therefore, and teach all nations, baptizing them in the name of the Father, and of the Son, and of the Holy Ghost: teaching them to observe all things whatsoever I have commanded you: and, lo, I am with you always, even unto the end of the world. Amen" (Matt. 28:19).

Stephen preached against sin and corruption in the church, and because of his preaching he was stoned to death. The apostle Paul wrote spiritual letters to these churches and preached against corruption in the churches, and of course when Paul was Saul he persecuted Christians until the Holy Spirit knocked him off his high horse. In fact, in many instances these churches functioned for the vanity pleasure of men, not the glory of God. Identical problems exist in twenty-first-century churches. God made it *right* in the first century. God will make it *right* in the twenty-first century.

The prayer of every man, woman, and child should be: "Lord, have mercy upon me a sinner: help me not to participate in any form of corrupting the church of Jesus Christ. Help me to become a part of Your glory in the church of Jesus Christ. Heavenly Father, teach me how to love pastors but fall in love with Jesus, because falling in love with Jesus is the best thing that could happen to any individual." Jesus is the Sword of God's Truth. "Think not that I come to send peace on earth. I came not to send peace, but a sword" (Matt. 10:34). Jesus in this passage declares war. *The war is a spiritual one: love versus hate and the truth versus a lie.*

"For though we walk in the flesh, we do not war after the flesh: for the weapons of our warfare are not carnal, but mighty through God to the pulling down of strong holds; casting down imaginations, and every high thing that exalteth itself against the knowledge of God, and bringeth into captivity every thought to the obedience of Christ; and having in a readiness to revenge all disobedience, when your obedience is fulfilled" (2 Cor. 10:3–6). *Individuals who say peace, peace without moral order simply do not understand peace.* We cannot have peace on earth without moral order. Jesus declared that "My mother, father, sisters, and brothers are those who love God/Truth and do the will of God."

The Christian church in America should be the one institution that serves as a critical *moral* apparatus that stands in judgment on the aims and conduct of secular society. In my opinion the public sector role of the church is to apply *moral accountability pressure* on secular leadership and institutional structures. Far too many individuals in leadership positions do not want to be accountable but rather desire to play God, that is *be footloose and fancy-free,* not responsible for decision outcomes. Ungodly conformity is the order of the day rather than accountability either to God or to others. The first order of accountability is to God and His principles, precepts, and concepts. American culture is on the *decline morally, politically, and* economically.

Indeed, it is funny how mentally and spiritually anything and everything goes in America. We must stop the mental and spiritual abuse of one another before we can become the nation the founding fathers envisioned: *(a) we hold these truths to be self-evident that all men are created equal and (b) in God we trust.* We have an abundance of materialistic stuff; therefore if the American dream is simply about *materialism* we are not in decline but on the rise, because banks are bursting at the seams with money and the rich are getting richer.

Unfortunately, because of double-minded Christian leadership the church does not function in the role of *just institutional arbiter* between right and wrong. Relativism makes right wrong for after all justice is a worldly human concept, but God says we reap what we sow. The double-minded Christian leadership style has ushered more worldly influence into the church than godly influence into the world. In short, there is more world in the church than church in the world. These circumstances exist because too many pastoral leaders enjoy living the contradiction. But they should know that they have a double portion coming from God:

> My brethren, be not many masters, knowing that we shall receive the greater condemnation. For in many things we offend all. If any man offends not in word, the same is a perfect man, and able also to bridle the whole body.
>
> James 3:1–2

The teaching and preaching of the gospel of Good News is not a job but a total commitment to God, a higher calling—a higher purpose!

CHRISTIAN LEADERSHIP: SACREDNESS VS. PROFANENESS

What does the Bible say about *Christian* leadership? What does the Bible say about pastoral leadership? Church leadership has not changed very much from the first century to the twenty-first century. In the first century, Jesus chased the *moneychangers* out of the Temple. Today the capitalists/entrepreneurs (*moneychangers*) are back and stronger than ever. The book of 3 John was written as a personal letter of encouragement to Gaius concerning members of a local church beset with leadership problems, especially Diotrephes, the self-proclaimed church leader. The role of church leadership is to lead individuals to Christ through examples of godly living. How church leaders live and conduct themselves before others is of critical importance, because leaders' behavior often influences the spiritual growth of believers and determines whether a church has a dynamic "Great Commission" ministry in Christ (Matt. 28:19; Mark 16:15–16).

Instead of embracing the Great Commission, many pastoral leaders embrace the "limited commission" and enslave church members to them in a local community. Ultimately these pastoral leaders make the church *their* church, rather than the church of Jesus Christ. Pastors have been instructed by *Christ Jesus* to teach parishioners to observe all things whatsoever *He* has commanded them. "Teaching them to observe all things whatsoever I have commanded you: and, lo, I am with you always, even unto the end of the world. Amen" (Matt. 28:20).

How an individual treats others is a true reflection of their value system—that is a measurement of what is importance to an individual. Are people simply things or objects to be used? Or are they unique creations of a loving God? Gaius was an individual known for his Christian hospitality and generosity. He followed the teachings of Jesus and loved and served others. Diotrephes loved to take the preeminence of leadership over the church: *I am the man.* John said: "Wherefore, if I come, I will remember his deeds which he doeth, prating against us with malicious words: and not content therewith, neither doth he himself receive the brethren, and forbiddeth them that would, and casteth them out of the church" (3 John 1:10).

Unfortunately, in the twenty-first century too many pastoral leaders are following the same course of action as Diotrephes did, embracing the self-centered model of leadership rather than the servanthood model. This is precisely why we have so many self-serving storefront ministries in urban communities preying on the poor. Some of these individuals come out of physical prisons and end up creating spiritual prisons for themselves as well as others.

What Makes a Preacher a Pastor?

Maybe people *select* preachers but God *chooses* (anoints) pastors after *His* own heart. Paul expresses the issue in this manner: "Let every man abide in the same calling wherein he was called. Art thou called being a servant?

Care not for it: but if thou mayest be made free, use it rather. For he that is called in the Lord, *being* a servant, is the Lord's freeman: likewise also he that is called, being free, is Christ servant. Ye are bought with a price: be not the servants of men. Brethern, let every man, wherein he is called, therein abide with God" (1 Corinthians 7: 20–24). Therefore "many are called, but few are chosen." A pastor of a church has one central role and that is to teach individuals how to have a personal *spiritual* relationship with God, Jesus, and the Holy Spirit. An individual can only teach that which he knows. The difference between being a preacher and a pastor is like the difference between being *good* versus being *godly*.

Even though King Saul was anointed by God he chose to be *goodly* rather than *godly*. The personal power struggle between King Saul and David was about character development. "The Lord therefore be judge, and judge between me and thee, and see, and plead my cause, and deliver me out of thine hand. And it came to pass, when David had made an end of speaking these words unto Saul, that Saul said, Is this thy voice, my son David? And Saul lifted up his voice, and wept. And he said to David, Thou art more righteous than I: for thou hast rewarded me with good, whereas I have rewarded thee evil" (1 Sam. 24:15–19).

David was *godly* but got off track lusting after Uriah's wife, Bathsheba. All of us sin and fall short of the glory of God, even a man after God's own heart. After Saul sinned against God and David, we hear nothing else about King Saul. However, after David sinned against God, Uriah, and Bathsheba, we know that after a long personal struggle God forgave David, and consequently *God states that David was a man after His own heart.*

Preaching is about homiletics and style. A pastor is *anointed* by God to preach and teach the Word in and out of season. The proof of a pastor's anointing is in how the congregation responds or relates to the Word of God. If an anointed pastor preaches and teaches the Word, invariably he/she will save souls. Without a doubt, *every God-called pastor has had*

a Damascus road experience. God has to knock you off your wheels-high ass,
which in modern times simply means your expensive car. A Damascus road
experience means an individual has been to Calvary, looked over on
the other side, and seen the glory of God in all its majesty. Dr. Martin
Luther King Jr. had such an experience prior to his murder. This why
Dr. King could declare "I am not afraid of dying."

To be sure, pastors must lead and serve with love and service;
preachers more often than not preach for money. Preaching is one
thing; servant leadership is a *God-thing.* Jesus is the Good Shepherd
and an anointed pastor is a good under-shepherd. "I am the good
shepherd: the good shepherd giveth his life for the sheep" (John 10:11).
A preacher is a hireling: self-called or so-called. Jesus had harsh words for
these individuals: "But he that is a hireling, and not the shepherd whose
own the sheep are not, seeth the wolf coming, and leaveth the sheep,
and fleeth; and the wolf catcheth them, and scattereth the sheep. The
hireling fleeth, because he is a hireling, and careth not for the sheep"
(John 10:11–12). To reiterate, pastoring is not a *job* it is a commitment
one makes to God. "As a servant earnestly desireth the shadow and as a
hireling looketh for the reward of his work" (Job 7:2).

Preaching and teaching are not about hustling and pimping.
Unfortunately, too many preachers masquerade as pastors when in fact
they are simply good corporate businessmen, because in many instances
they have turned churches into successful individualistic corporations:
the "my church" syndrome. These so-called churches have become the
epitome of what is commonly called trickle-down economics.

Therefore, every Christian believer is expected to grow spiritually
and become a *worthy* leader by example: "But grow in grace, and in the
knowledge of our Lord and Savior Jesus Christ. To him be glory both
now and forever. Amen" (2 Pet. 3:18). *Jesus must receive the glory now*
and forevermore, not the pastor or any other human. When the burden
of Christian leadership rests solely upon the shoulders of pastors, the

temptation for *hero worship* becomes magnified and sometimes even glorified—and people forget that only to God be the glory, honor, praise, and power for He created all things. "Thou art worthy, O Lord, to receive glory and honor and power: for thou hast created all things, and for thy pleasure they are and were created" (Rev. 4:11).

Pastoral hero-worship has become a central overriding problem in twenty-first-century Christian leadership. But what does the Word of God tell us? "It is better to trust in the Lord than to put confidence in man" (Ps. 18:8). God is the *only hero*, and if an individual is not careful he/she might become a *zero* seeking to become a *hero*, because of *ego-tripping*.

The Bible warns us against trusting others with our spiritual *soul* salvation; every individual is responsible for his/her own soul salvation, including pastors. "For we must all appear before the judgment seat of Christ; that every one may receive the things done in his body, according to that he hath done, whether it be good or bad" (2 Cor. 5:10). This state of worldly vanity has led too many pastoral leaders to elevate ministry to the level and trappings of celebrity status: bodyguards, servants, expensive cars, castles on hills, and fine jewelry. Rather than walk in the precepts of our Lord and Savior Jesus Christ, these pastors choose to glorify themselves with things. God has already fixed the church; our task as Christian believers is to allow the church to be the church and to stop trying to fix our *bank accounts* using the church as the monetary instrument.

"But it is written, Eye hath not seen, nor ear heard, neither have entered into the heart of man, the things which God hath prepared for them that love him" (1 Cor. 2:9). Loving *self-glorification* is dangerous for both pastors and parishioners. "For all have sinned, and come short of the glory of God; being justified freely by his grace through the redemption that is in Christ Jesus" (Rom. 3:23). "Neither is there salvation in any other: for there is none other name under heaven given among men, whereby we must be saved" (Acts 4:12). While the church is an institution like all other institutions in society, because of its purpose the church is duty-bound to think in spiritual terms but act in political terms without embracing partisan politics. This is the only effective approach if the church is to realize the Great Commission: saving souls. This approach minimizes the temptation for pastors to want to act like politicians. For as Christians we must be in the world but not of the world. Thinking in spiritual terms helps to keep the church spiritually grounded.

PRAYER

God, our heavenly Father, we know that in the fullness of time You will gather together all things in Jesus Christ in heaven and on earth. Therefore, for Your goodness and mercy we give You praise because You have truly blessed America. We pray that America now bless You, heavenly Father, because all things shall be placed at the feet of Jesus simply because Jesus is the Head of the church, which is His body and the fullness of Him who fills all in all. We know that Jesus is the Sword of the Truth; therefore don't let the Sword catch any Christian believer on the wrong side—the non-redemption side—when it comes. In the name of Jesus is our humble prayer. Let the church be the church. Get right, church. The King of Kings is coming. Amen!

Chapter 4

BLENDING CHRISTIANITY INTO EDUCATIONAL PROCESSES

Blessed is he that readeth, and they that hear the words of this prophecy, and keep those things which are written therein: for the time is at hand.

Revelation 1:3

"Go to the ant, thou sluggard; consider her ways, and be wise: which having no guide, overseer or ruler, provideth her meat in the summer, and gathereth her food in the harvest. How long wilt thou sleep, O sluggard? When wilt thou arise out of thy sleep?" (Prov. 6:6–9). Indeed, ants seemingly build a greater sense of community and orderliness than do human beings. God has declared that as humans we can learn from observing animals and nature.

The wisdom of the founding fathers is most vividly expressed in the establishment of a *mass public educational system*; simply because social democracy requires a spiritually enlightened and educated population. Social democracy is human beings seeking to work out *ethical-moral* resource allocation: mindset for a *just* society. The battle for *justice* is fought in the mind (thoughts). Formal education then is the basis for a *just* democratic society, not necessarily a *spiritual* society. Furthermore, the Bible declares that the person who can read is blessed, because it is through reading that an individual acquires knowledge and wisdom, which is the pathway to understanding.

"According as his divine power hath given unto us all things that pertain unto life and godliness, through the knowledge of him that hath called us to glory and virtue: Whereby are given unto us exceeding great and precious promises: that by these ye might be partakers of the divine nature, having escaped the corruption that is in the world through lust" (2 Pet. 1:3–4). Everything an individual needs to know about life and life more abundantly is in the *BOOK*: the Bible. Education is about critical thinking, or intellectual integrity. Integrity is the basis for moral character development.

What has made America a great nation is its commitment to education for the masses, not just education for the elite. Of course, this is why people come from all around the world to America to acquire a "quality" education. In part, it is access to an education that helps fuel immigration as well as the notion of world citizenship. An individual can *legally* immigrate, learn to speak the language (English), understand the rules of social interaction (laws), and become an American. Unfortunately, there are numerous countries on planet earth were this process does not exist.

All knowledge, wisdom, and understanding come from God. The categories of understanding—time, class, space, and number—are *original spiritual concepts* in the Bible. This is primarily why the founders desired that people be able to read in order that they might be able to *read* and *comprehend* the Bible. Formalized educational development is based upon these biblically based concepts. Without a doubt, formal educational development plays a key role in both individual and societal development. God created individuals as free moral agents with freedom of will. The devil does not like freedom but loves bondage because he does not want individuals to experience freedom. The devil's objective is slavery to sin and wrongdoing. In fact, he desires that sin (wrongdoing) be legalized. As humans with a free will we enslave ourselves when we make bad, unrighteous, and immoral decisions simply because decisions (choices) have consequences, good or evil.

The basis for morality is *God-consciousness*, and of course laws should reflect a sense of *godly* morality, not devilish immorality. This is why most of our criminal and civil law codes are based upon the Ten Commandments, or the notion of a moral absolute. God is the only absolute; therefore God is the only constant eternal basis for morality and social moral order. Hence, formal education is what helps us learn how to make positive enlightened life choices so that we might experience positive consequences: results.

To reiterate, the breakdown of the family unit in American society has had a devastating impact on educational institutions and administrative processes as well as student development at every level. We live in a fatherless society, especially in the black community, and to a lesser degree in other ethnic minority communities. Therefore, it is indeed unfortunate that public schooling has not adjusted its *structure* to accommodate the needs of children who come from one-parent families. All children have biological fathers, but few have daddies in the home. This social fact alone adversely affects the nature of public schooling. In order to be effective, public schooling must be able to function as a *surrogate* family structure given the current state of affairs.

Without a doubt, the teaching and training of children in behavioral manners is the responsibility of parents. The reality is stark: many children enter the public schooling process undisciplined and without the emotional intelligence to sit in a structured classroom environment and behave appropriately. To a large degree, all education is about moral education and character development. In ethnic communities, the outward trappings of religion play an important role in communal life. Hence, public schooling should reflect a sense of moral order, internalized self-discipline, and sacredness, not just secular worldliness. Most teachers spend 80 percent of their time trying to maintain classroom order without the management tool of corrective discipline. When families fail to teach children behavioral manners and emotional intelligence, the responsibility then shifts to the public schooling process. Of course, society should not expect teachers to maintain classroom order without giving them the management tool of corrective discipline. Teachers do not have time to discipline children, only teach children. "Withhold not correction from the child: for if thou beatest him with the rod, he shall not die. Thou shalt beat him with the rod, and shalt deliver his soul from hell" (Prov. 23:13–14). There is an old commonsense biblically based adage: "Spare the rod, spoil the child."

The message here is not about spanking advocacy or corporal punishment but biblical expository. Personally, I sought to values-orient my children toward the way of the Lord in freewill self-discipline. Parents cannot be with their children 24/7. It is more desirable for parents to discipline children with love than for police officers to discipline children with the legal authority of the club and the gun. Again, my parenting style was based primarily upon helping my children learn how to exercise internal self-discipline rather than me always having to discipline them externally. This approach worked for me but not for my wife. To reiterate the biblical point of view: "Train up a child in the way he should go and when he is old he will not depart from it" (Prov. 22:6).

Even though I exercised discipline in my home, I wanted my daughters to understand that a man should not physically abuse or punish a female child because sometimes girls grow up thinking that it is okay for a man to physically discipline a woman. This can lead to men physically abusing women, and of course this is sin. The *spiritual lesson* I sought to teach all three of my children is simply this: godly parents discipline with love. Policemen discipline with clubs and guns, backed up by societal laws.

The antisocial behaviors associated with our children begin in the home, not the school. God, the Bible, prayer, and the rod all have been taken out of the school environment, and the devil and his angels rule the school through undisciplined children because our children are listening to the prince of the air on television, the Internet, Facebook, iPads, video games, music videos, and so on. If society is willing to err, it should err on the side of good, because God is good and the Bible as a guide is good.

American society has allowed *public schooling* to become morally degenerate. "Yet I had planted thee a noble vine, wholly a right seed: how then art thou turned into the degenerate plant of a strange vine unto me?" (Jer. 2:21). The question is: what happened? Could it be that taking God, the Bible, prayer, and the rod out of schools might be the answer? There is no divine moral authority in schools, only humankind's conception of the meaning of life. Evolution/revolution = no solution.

Therefore, in the current public schooling systems, both teachers and students are frustrated. In the educational developmental process all things must work together for those who love children. Administrators, teachers, and support staff must foster love, dedication, and service as the foundation of public schooling. Public schooling must not simply become a paycheck system. If so, then our nation is doomed because the very foundation of social democracy is held hostage by the greed factor. Public schooling must be based upon the philosophy of children first; then we leave no child behind. "No child left behind" is only half the equation. Public schools must find creative ways to address the single-parent-family issue by providing parenting-skills classes in the evenings. "No parent left behind" completes the equation: *No child left behind; no parent left behind.*

To reiterate, there must be *B*asic *I*nstruction *B*efore *L*eaving *E*arth: knowledge of the *Bible*. This spiritual concept of life must be taught and embraced by children before leaving home to attend public school, and of course reinforced by the church. Scientifically, from a *human development* point of view, everything a child needs to know about life, he/she learns from birth to age six. These are the most valuable formative learning years for every child's development. If these early childhood years are dysfunctional the average child probably will not succeed in school.

Independent school districts are compelled to employ full-time police officers to maintain superficial *physical* moral order because *internal* moral order must be fostered in the home. Far too many of the nation's children have been negatively impacted mentally and psychologically by growing up in one-parent households. Many of these mothers, already under stress from shouldering the responsibilities of work and childrearing without a husband, participate in antisocial behaviors such as alcohol consumption, smoking, and doping. The devastating aftereffect is children born with mental and psychological issues, which in turn adversely affects their ability to sit in structured learning environments. Of course, the end result is medicated children and a medicated society. The cultural devastation for society in the long run is a subpopulation of individuals who are instant-gratification oriented.

"For by grace are ye saved through faith; and not of yourselves: it is the gift of God: not of works, least any man should boast. For we are his workmanship, created in Christ Jesus unto good works, which God hath before ordained that we should walk in them" (Eph. 2:8–9). Work is also divine thoughts/motives, acts, and actions. "For as he thinketh in his heart, so is he" (Prov. 23:7a). Of course, "Be not wise in thine own eyes; hear the Lord, and depart from evil" (Prov. 3:7). This ungodly instant-gratification philosophy has produced a subculture of individuals who do not understand that *work is the ultimate form of self-gratification, because work is one of God's gifts to us.* God works 24/7—even the night shift. God sacrificed His only begotten Son so that our souls might be saved from eternal damnation: hell.

God worked *six* days and rested on the *seventh* day. In my opinion, too many teachers have turned public schooling into a paycheck system. God's work is not about materialistic pay. Likewise the work of Jesus was not about materialistic pay. Jesus' work was about love and service. Therefore the work of teachers should be about love and service. "And on the seventh day God ended His work which he had made: and he rested on the seventh day from all his work which he had made" (Gen. 2:2). If God worked, what then about us? Jesus said: "So after he had washed their feet, and had taken his garments, and was set down again, he said unto them, Know ye what I have done to you? Ye call me master and Lord: and ye say well; for so I am. If I then, your Lord and Master, have washed your feet; ye also ought to wash one another's feet. For I have given you an example, that ye should do as I have done to you" (John 13:12–15).

To Jesus the church was about love and service. The effectiveness of the church can only be measured by the community in which it exists. If the church community is rundown, dogs running loose, garbage not being picked and sorted, ungodly activities abound. Then it can be said that the church is not effective in the community. "And on the seventh day God ended his work which he had made; and he rested on the seventh day from all of his work which he had made" (Gen. 2:2). Meaningful work is ultimate self-fulfillment. "And about the eleventh hour he went out, and found others standing idle, he said unto them, why stand ye all the day idle? They say unto him, because no man has hired us. He saith unto them, go ye also into the vineyard; and whatsoever is right, that ye shall receive" (Matt. 20: 6–9).

In the public schooling process all things must work together for those who love children, because children are the future. Of course, without a vision for the future we perish. The ability to read and comprehend is the foundational key to educational success. Therefore reading is the universally proven process that enhances educational development. The proven way of learning how to read is *phonics* and the Bible. I learned how to read from the Bible in church-school at the age of four. Church schoolteachers and Sunday school teachers were learned individuals.

Too many minority children are failing state/national standardized tests because they cannot read, comprehend, or write. Sadly, effective teaching oftentimes does not take place because teachers have to contend with discipline issues. Achievement tests are important evaluation tools. Standardized tests are based upon middle-class values, and many ethnic-minority students are not acquainted with middle-class values constructs; therefore these children may not understand how important *social conduct* is to completing high school and becoming a productive citizen. There is no such thing as education without *corrective discipline*. Teachers cannot teach in chaotic and immoral school environments. Oftentimes minority children *do not understand* the structural connection between public school and society in general, especially the world of work.

Lack of parental involvement (accountability) in the educational/ developmental process of children is a key factor in the declining quality of public schooling. This horrible state of affairs has fueled a movement on the part of *some* free-enterprise opportunists to seek to privatize education: *charter schools*. The privatization of education is anti-social democracy. The business of schooling is human development, not capitalism—that is making profits. Privatizing education is not the solution to the problems plaguing public schooling.

The major influences on child development have changed over time, producing a generation gap based upon moral values. Indeed, values are priorities. What primarily influences human development is what an individual values as priorities. Scientific social research has established that in the 1950s home, school, church, peers, and television influenced child development, in that order. The Bible declares that every generation becomes wiser and at the same time more wicked. In the 1980s there was a dramatic shift in influence impact on child development, with the order being home, peers, television, school, and church. In the 1990s the influence ordering was peers, television, home-media, school, and church. In the twenty-first century the influence ordering is different media types: Videos, Internet, computers, movies, and network television—in short, nothing sacred, everything secular.

Technology has turned children into *kids* with an *each to his own way philosophy and approach to life*. I do my thing, you do your thing. It is extremely difficult to teach *kids* who want to do their own thing. The motivation to learn must come from within (internal desire and self-motivation), fostered and nurtured within the family context. Unfortunately, today's *kids* are accustomed to being entertained rather than spiritually/educationally enlightened. The foundation for creative living is self-motivation. It is much easier to teach disciplined individuals than it is to teach undisciplined individuals. And it is much more pleasant and rewarding for teachers to teach children who have been taught the *way of the Lord by their parents*. Discipline is learning to do things decently and in order. "Let all things be done decently and in order" (1 Cor. 14:40).

SCHOOL CHOICE:
PRIVATIZATION VS. DEMOCRATIZATION

Providing a quality education for all children is the civil rights issue of the twenty-first century, not same-sex marriage. Of course, *voting rights* are of equal importance. Civil rights and voting rights are synonymous. In some instances individuals were imprisoned to strip them of their legal civil rights to prevent the exercise of voting rights. Citizenship is the basis for voting rights. To be effective, democracy requires an enlightened, spiritually grounded, and well-educated citizenry.

While the intent of school choice and charter schools in general was noble and well-intentioned, the process of implementing in many instances left a lot to be desired. The legislation that created the impetus for school choice/charter school districts was flawed. In some instances, individuals who received charters were primarily interested in profits and personal gain, not the educational development of children. Many of the individuals holding state charters are not professional educators but rather small business entrepreneurs (mom-and-pop style) seeking to privatize taxpayer dollars for personal profits. *Oftentimes, and in many vulgar and sundry ways, they seek to transform non-profit into profit.* Of course, this ungodly process leaves both children and parents behind.

In the Houston Independent School District (HISD), one of the largest urban school districts in the United States, approximately 8 percent of the children are white. The question is why. Because far more than 8 percent of the Houston Independent School District's residential service population is white. As of 2011, 50 percent to 66 percent of the white students within HISD's boundaries were enrolled in private schools. The majority population in HISD is Hispanic, at 61 percent. Blacks comprise 26 percent of the students enrolled in HISD.

Former Governor George Wallace of Alabama stood in the schoolhouse door and declared: "Segregation today, segregation tomorrow, and segregation forever." The question is, is school segregation today accidental or planned by design? If children do not learn together how can they learn to live together? Separate education helps to facilitate a separate, unequal, and unjust society. Unfortunately, all children do not begin the public schooling process on a level playing field. Some children are blessed to grow up in healthy developmental environments, and of course other children are less fortunate because of bad parenting decisions.

One question comes to mind: is the notion of school choice, vouchers, and charter schools simply a sophisticated way to privatize the education of whites and segregate public schools at the expense of taxpayers? Or is this process just about *money* and social class? Or does this process make the George Wallace declaration a self-fulfilling prophecy? The affluent will always be able to provide private education for their children, and of course that is to be expected, but not at the expense of taxpayers: *vouchers.*

In a capitalistic society there are many layers of social class, but primarily there are four: upper class, middle class, working class, and the poor. Social-class positioning determines access to valued societal resources, including a quality education. Therefore the concept of vouchers has simply become a means for middle-class parents to provide a private school environment for their children at taxpayers' expense. Moreover, no one should have a problem with how individuals choose to educate their children or spend their money as long as it is their money, not taxpayer money. The voucher system was initiated by middle-class individuals for middle-class individuals.

To be sure, we do not choose our parents or their socioeconomic position in society. Some are given privileges based solely upon ethnic and racial identity. We still have not reached the Promised Land because racial and ethnic institutional divisions still exist. One of God's gifts to human beings is sexuality. Therefore we should be careful how we deal with the gift, because free will is the *gift* of gifts. Simply put, if a society cannot integrate ideas about the meaning of life, then a society cannot integrate cultures and bodies.

The 1954 Supreme Court decision *Brown v. Board of Education* did not allow for strategy implementation input by blacks or browns (minorities). The method of implementation, "forced bussing," created white flight and ultimately contributed to the process of destroying public schools in minority neighborhoods. Unfortunately, public schools in minority communities to this day have not fully recovered from the impact of *forced bussing* primarily because of funding issues and teacher quality.

The idea of school choice should be a creative avenue for improving educational quality. But in many instances the legislation that created charter school districts was policy flawed and helped fuel the privatization process of public education, because oversight state educational agencies did not think through unintended consequences.

The best example of a public school system creatively responding to the competition of school choice is the Washington, D.C., public schools. In 1981 voters in the District of Columbia public schools considered a ballot initiative to bring widespread school choice to public schools. The initiative was defeated by a 9 to 1 vote. In the 30 years since that vote, as many as 50,000 students have dropped out of the D.C. public schools. In fact, 30 years later parents are giving school choice a second look, and as a result sweeping reforms are occurring throughout D.C. public schools. Today D.C. has as many as 57 charter schools, enrolling more than 31,562 students. In addition, over 1584 students attend private schools using vouchers through a federally funded Opportunity Scholarship Program. When creatively thought through, educational competition and school choice sometimes can improve educational quality. School choice did improve the District of Columbia's public school system.

When all is said and done, public schools should always be the *first choice* but not necessarily the only choice, because there are some children who fall through the educational cracks in traditional public schools for various reasons. School choice does provide options for these students who otherwise might end up as dropouts and ultimately dysfunctional members of society. But unfortunately in the school choice scheme of things too often the choice is for vulgar profits for small-minded capitalistic profiteers, not quality education for children. The greed factor has been intellectualized and institutionalized in a capitalistic society. There is absolutely nothing good about greed, because greed is ungodly. The story of the man who wanted to tear down his barns and build bigger barns is an everlasting example of the dangers of greed (Luke 12:18). The price tag on greed is your soul. Or the price tag just might be too big to fail.

DEDICATED TEACHERS VS. COMPUTER TECHNOLOGY

Teaching is a godly vocational commitment. Jesus was called a great teacher sent from God. Indeed, Jesus was the greatest teacher that ever lived, simply because He taught by example. Education is about creative thinking ability and human interaction. Oftentimes computers inhibit creative thinking ability, attention span, teacher-student interaction, and hands-on learning by students, and of course it should not be that way. Both teachers and technology should work in concert for best educational results. Teachers teach, not machines. Machines can do only what they have been programmed to do. "Happy is the man that findeth wisdom, and the man that getteth understanding" (Prov. 3:13).

The Bible declares: "For as he thinketh in his heart, so is he: Eat and drink, saith he to thee; but his heart is not with thee" (Prov. 23:7). Conversely, the machine has no spiritual human quality and therefore to eat bread (knowledge/understanding) from the machine *might* be evil because it is of man, not God. "Eat thou not the bread of him that hath an evil eye, neither desire thou his dainty meats" (Prov. 23:6). Of course, "Shall not God search this out? For he knoweth the secrets of the heart" (Ps. 44:21). For God knows: "The heart is deceitful above all things, and desperately wicked: who can know it?" (Jer. 17:9). The answer is *but God.* "I the Lord search the heart, I try the reins, even to give every man according to his ways, and according to the fruit of his doings" (Jer. 17:10).

You shall reap what you so: *the laws of reciprocity.* "Be not deceived; God is not mocked: for whatsoever man soweth, that shall he also reap. For he that soweth to his flesh shall of the flesh reap corruption; but he that soweth to the spirit shall of the spirit reap life everlasting" (Gal. 6:7–8).

Technology should not take the place of highly qualified and well-trained teachers because teachers inspire, not technology. Teachers must teach children how to think analytically. Technology is a teaching assistance tool. Teaching is about human interaction or teacher-student relationships. Hence, teaching is an enterprise of the mind. Technology is created by human minds; hence the ability to think is the basis for creative living, not technology. In fact, if we are not careful as a society technology will orient human mindset toward objects rather than people.

Technology can edge God out, but teachers can include God. In fact, teachers can include God without calling upon the name of God through setting godly examples. Teachers can teach and example godly love; machines cannot. It is truly a difficult task to teach those whom you do not love. For after all, this is the manner in which Jesus taught in the Temple as a young child. But, more importantly, education is the key to a healthy democratic society. Albert Einstein said, "I fear the day that technology will surpass our *human interaction.* The world will have a generation of idiots." When we strip ourselves of humanistic values and instincts we leave ourselves vulnerable to machines as well as the wiles of the devil. Becoming a slave to technology is definitely not a good thing.

I entered college with a burning desire to become a public schoolteacher. My undergraduate degree is in education, inspired by the wonderful public schoolteachers who taught me from kindergarten through the twelfth grade. I remember all my teachers to this very day, including the principal: Rudolph Perry Dawkins. I fondly remember all my teachers for three very important reasons. First, all of them demonstrated that they loved me. Secondly, they demonstrated that they wanted the best life had to offer for me, and they were willing to help me acquire the necessary skills to achieve personal life goals. Thirdly, they were the only adults in classrooms and required that everyone behave appropriately, and of course this was reinforced by your family. The students who got *twisted* quickly got *untwisted* because of positive peer group influence. Without a doubt, every student received the message and behaved appropriately.

I might add that the majority of the teachers who taught me were women. In the past women had limited earning power opportunities; therefore teaching was one of the few opportunities available to them. In the twenty-first century this is true to a lesser degree. Most of these women were highly intelligent, the cream of the crop. Over the years I have concluded that women are more effective teachers in public school settings than men, especially kindergarten through eighth grades. Of course, this is not to say that men cannot be effective teachers in grades K–8. In my opinion women can more easily transition the roles of teacher and mother (nurturing) than men are able to transition the roles of teacher and father figure.

Unfortunately, many men want to get too macho in public school settings. I am not saying that men at the K–8 levels cannot be effective teachers. Indeed an authoritarian fair-minded male teacher is able to maintain respect at a high level through *tough love and fear of consequences.* Women tend to rule with love and reasoning. Men tend to rule with fear and discipline. Men usually make clear that there are consequences for behavior. Men and women are wired differently. Men have to learn how to mother (nurture) women and women must learn how to father (strengthen) men. Difference should not equate to sexism: discrimination and social inequities.

The institutional church has failed to magnify God's Word and glorify God spiritually. In so doing, confusion is rampant in the church as well as in public education, rather than reasoning and spiritual/ internal discipline. This state of affairs has produced: (a) lack of godly discipline in the home, (b) lack of godly discipline in the classroom, and (c) ungodliness in society, or social chaos. "What? Know ye not that your body is the temple of the Holy Ghost which is in you, which ye have of God, and ye are not your own? For ye are bought with a price: therefore glorify God in your body, and in your spirit, which are God's" (1 Cor. 6:19–20).

Unfortunately, our children are not taught this profound spiritual truth either in the home, church, or society in general. So many children enter public schools with limited self-disciplinary understanding, and as a result confusion is the order of the day. This sad state of affairs has led to our children becoming lawless because they do not know the Lawgiver, and invariably *bad attitudes place bricks on prison walls.*

Dedicated teachers are motivated to nurture and example before children four basic social characteristics: *desire,* which is an internal state of being; *ability,* a realistic skill set; *support,* a team teaching approach designed to inspire students toward high expectations; and *confidence,* teachers helping students acquire the attitude that "I can do all things through Jesus Christ who strengthens me." *Yes I Can.* For after all, life is about attitude. A positive attitude determines aptitude, or the propensity for individuals to learn the right thing(s) rather than the wrong thing(s). Aptitude determines altitude—how high an individual will go in life.

Education is not a partisan political issue; it is the essential foundation of a healthy democratic society. The founding fathers believed this to be true and so should Americans in the twenty-first century.

A quality education helps an individual learn how to fish so that he might be able to save him/herself as well as help others. "Blessed is he that readeth, and they that hear the words of this prophecy, and keep those things which are written therein: for the time is at hand" (Rev. 1:3).

PRAYER

We pray, heavenly Father, that the mind which was in Jesus Christ be in all of us, especially our children. We thank You for Your loving mercy because Jesus is a real friend. We pray for the right direction for our children as well as the nation's future. Lord, we need a clarion call from heaven to young men and women so that they might embrace the gospel of Jesus Christ. Our prayer is that this godly clarion call be as clear in the twenty-first century as it was in the first century. For in times like these America needs godly leadership in our homes, churches, schools, political institutions, and business institutions. We pray, heavenly Father, that You guide and direct each American to embrace godly principles and godly examples of leadership. Let the church be the church. Get right, church. The King of Kings is coming. Amen!

Chapter 5

BLENDING CHRISTIANITY INTO POLITICS AND GOVERNMENT

Righteousness exalteth a nation: but sin is a reproach to any people.

Proverbs 14:34

In every social movement for righteousness in American history, Christian churches were at the forefront to some degree—on the side of what is right in relationship to God's Word. The question is: where has the church gone? Conscience is a valuable human commodity. Of course, love and service are important realities because love and service come from a righteous conscience. To be sure, the road to hell is paved with good intentions. Therefore it is not enough to have good intentions; good intentions must be translated into moral action: love and service.

Jesus did not build a fence around the concept of neighbor. It has been said that fences make good neighbors. However, not everyone agrees—including me. Fences create confusion rather than moral unity. Likewise, four walls cannot contain God or the church of Jesus Christ. The institutional church is simply a place where believing saints come together to praise and worship God, thanking Him for His grace, forgiveness, and mercy and to hear the Word of God spoken. Without a doubt, God's divine way of communicating with individuals is always through conscience.

The Christian church is not morally integrated—flesh and spirit—and so American society is not morally integrated. To reiterate, the Christian church should be the foundation of societal truth and moral order. Yet eleven o'clock on Sunday morning is the most segregated hour in American society. We do not worship God in spirit and truth together in churches, and non-spiritual-minded individuals keep us from being buried together in graveyards and cemeteries. Hence, since we are not spiritually unified as one nation under God, even in death we cannot rest in peace. Seemingly, from the womb to the tomb we are not morally unified and integrated as a righteous society. This is precisely why eleven o'clock on Sunday morning is still the most segregated hour in American society.

The church is to be the *spiritual* light of the world, not assist in perpetuating darkness and confusion. "Ye are the light of the world. A city that is set on a hill cannot be hid. Neither do men light a candlestick and put it under a bushel, but on a candlestick; and it giveth light unto all that are in the house. Let your light so shine before men, that they may see your good works, and glorify your Father which is in heaven" (Matt. 5:14–16).

As Christians we are commanded to keep our light and godly works shining brightly in the world. "Then spake Jesus again unto them, saying, I am the light of the world: he that followeth me shall not walk in darkness, but shall have the light of life" (John 8:12). And, "The light of the body is the eye: therefore when thine eye is single, thy whole body also is full of light; but when thine eye is evil, thy body also is full of darkness. Take heed therefore that the light which is in thee be not darkness. If thy whole body therefore be full of light, having no part dark, the whole shall be full of light, as when the bright shining of a candle doth give thee light" (Luke 11:34–36). The role of Christian leadership is to deliver the ungodly from darkness to light as Jesus commanded: "To open their eyes, and to turn them from darkness to light, and from the power of Satan unto God, that they may receive forgiveness of sins, and inheritance among them which are sanctified by faith that is in me" (Acts 26:18).

Yet we know that the established order of things is God, country, and family. This is the order the founding fathers envisioned for American society. God is first because all of us move and have our being in God. He is the reason why we wake up, not alarm clocks. If anyone thinks that an alarm clock can wake an individual up, take one to the graveyard, let it go off, and see how many dead people get up. It is God's love, grace, forgiveness, and mercy that wake individuals up every morning.

Of course, families should have a righteous country to live in, because righteousness exalts a nation. Hence, this is precisely why we say God, country, and family in this order. Government is about the needs of people: of the people, by the people, and for the people. Thus the Christian church must always speak the truth in love and with moral clarity, because speaking lies creates confusion rather than moral unity. The church should never become a silent majority but always embrace the truth in time, on time, and at all times.

Culturally we are engaged in fighting an *uncivilized* civil war based upon lies. If America is not careful the next revolution will not be televised, it will be silent, because it will be based upon lies. The Civil War of the 1860s was fought with guns, bayonets, and cannons in order to abolish chattel slavery. Its staggering cost in human lives was over 600,000. War is hell, because war is not an answer. In the 1970s Edwin Starr composed a song titled "WAR." In it he asked the question: "War, what is it good for?" Starr's answer: absolutely nothing! Individuals cannot kill the devil. Individuals cannot kill hatred. The Bible declares that there will always be wars and rumors of wars until Jesus returns. The question is why. War never solves *the* problem, but war does solve some problems for a short period of time—that is until the next war.

For example, the Civil War ended chattel slavery but did not resolve the problem of institutional racism: hatred. Former Governor of Alabama George Wallace declared that American society cannot legislate morality because morality begins with moral conscience, not law. The problem is a heart-and-mind problem, which is a spiritual problem: a God problem. War, therefore, is for killing. War cannot give life. War is good for the undertaker business. On the other hand Jesus says: "I come that you might have life and life more abundantly."

Morality, or moral order, begins and ends with God, not at the barrel of a gun. The Civil Rights movement of the 1960s ended legalized segregation and so-called separate but equal, that is desegregated public facilities. I believe President Lyndon B. Johnson is one of America's greatest presidents because of his bold moral leadership in this effort. Had it not been for his moral courage and moral leadership, the civil rights bill (1964) and the voting rights act (1965) probably would not have passed Congress. Both the Lincoln and Johnson eras in American history required strong, bold, and courageous moral leadership. Unfortunately, neither of these historic events created the moral integration of flesh and spirit in American society, primarily because the church failed to shoulder the burden of being the spiritual light of the nation.

Dr. Martin Luther King Jr.'s letter from the Birmingham jail sought to address the spiritual bankruptcy of the church in public life. Dr. King's philosophy concerning the role of the church was simple: *"If you see a just cause and a moral just fight is going on, get in the fight. If you see an injustice and there is no one who has started a moral just fight, then [you] start a fight."* Indeed the battle is the Lord's; the choice to get in the fight is about conscience. If an individual chooses to become a member of the *silent majority*, then he/she commits the sin of omission because he/she did not get in the fight for justice nor start one for justice (Matt. 23:23). Jesus refers to the sin of omission as the weightier matter of unrighteousness.

One of the primary roles of the church in society is to help usher in societal moral order: the moral integration of flesh and spirit. The church of Jesus Christ is not four walls but a spirit of love and service without walls. John the Baptist preached that the kingdom of God is here now: *the now-ness of life.* "Repent ye: for the kingdom of heaven is at hand" (Matt. 3:2). Jesus is the kingdom of God. Therefore every individual should shout hallelujah to the Lamb of God that takes away the sins of the world.

Institutional racism and sexism are debasements of our collective humanity and collective destiny as graveyard travelers because our humanity is grounded in the reality of God, not skin color or sex status. Too many so-called Christians enjoy living the contradiction simply for personal gain. To reiterate, these Christian believers have intellectualized that greed is good when the Bible defines greed, envy, and jealousy as sins (*works*) of the flesh and those who do such things cannot inherit the Kingdom of God (Galatians 5:19–26)."The blessing of the Lord, it maketh rich, and he added no sorrow with it" (Prov. 10: 22). The blessings of God make us rich when we seek first the kingdom of God; all other things will be added unto us.

Pastors have been commanded to preach the Word; therefore because the Word is being preached by some upside-down—that is twisted toward humankind and the things of this world rather than God—we have cultural churches rather than godly churches. This social fact is most clearly reflected in the musical styles in churches based upon emotionalism and the bottom line: *collection plates*. "Preach the word; be instant in season, out of season; reprove, rebuke, exhort with all long suffering and doctrine. For the time will come when they will not endure sound doctrine; but after their own lusts shall reap to themselves teachers, having itching ears; and shall turn away their ears from the truth, and shall be turned unto fables. But watch thou in all things, endure afflictions, do the work of an evangelist, make full proof of thy ministry" (2 Tim. 4:2–5).

But God says: "Let us therefore come boldly unto the throne of grace, that we may obtain mercy, and find grace to help us in time of need" (Heb. 4:16). We do not need cheerleaders or entertainers in our churches but God-fearing doctrinal teaching to help us in our spiritual walk with Jesus. Therefore, American society is not void of the reality of God, but void of sound biblical teaching.

How did we get in this horrible mess? More importantly, where do we go from here? What can the Christian tradition offer as solutions to the current moral, ecological, and environmental crises? Institutional Christianity is about individual responsibility, collective responsibility, stewardship, human values, and character development rather than godly spiritual values. We have a values problem: human exploitation and negative values. The moral failure of institutional Christianity has fueled the moral decline of American culture. Couple this social fact with our love of things and what you have is a recipe for societal chaos. Righteousness exalts a nation.

Overwhelmingly, too many Americans love things and use people, rather than loving people and using things as God commanded. Wealth without godliness is like laboring for the *wind*. "There is a sore evil which I have seen under the sun, namely, riches kept for the owners thereof to their hurt. But those riches perish by evil travail: and he begetteth a son, and there is nothing in his hand. As he came forth of his mother's womb, naked shall he return to go as he came, and shall take nothing of his labor, which he may carry away in his hand. And this also is a sore evil, that in all point as he came, so shall he go: and what profit hath he that hath labored for the wind? All his days also he eateth in darkness, and *he hath* much sorrow and wrath with his sickness" (Eccl. 5:13–17).

There is no harm in wealth and things if acquired through hard work, obedience, and the fear of God. However, *sinful* destruction is pronounced upon individuals who gain by means of greed, theft, and misappropriation.

> Behold that which I have seen: it is good and comely for one to eat and to drink, and to enjoy the good of all his labor that he taketh under the sun all the days of his life, which God giveth him: for it is his portion. Every man also to whom God hath given riches and wealth, and hath given him power to eat thereof, and to take his portion, and to rejoice in his labor; this is the gift of God. For he shall not much remember the days of his life; because God answereth him in the joy of his heart.
>
> **Ecclesiastes 5:20**

To reiterate, secular society has intellectualized and institutionalized greed. Institutional Christianity has sought to spiritualize greed: the prosperity gospel. Both are gross misrepresentations. Greed is greed.

In short, too many Americans have become exploiters of the creation, rather than *godlike caretakers*. Herein is the environmental crisis. God said: "And the land is defiled: therefore I do visit the iniquity thereof upon it, and the land itself vomiteth out her inhabitants" (Lev. 18:25). Our mindset is polluting the water we drink, the air we breathe, the food we eat, and above all how we live and relate to each other. Hence, the causes of the environmental crisis cannot be evaded forever because they are questions about individual as well as societal meaning. The questions are: How do we live? What are we willing to *sacrifice* to live the way we say we want to live? How do we transform collective interests into collective action? How do we learn to resolve conflict non-violently? How do we address the basic problem of *mindset* in relationship to how we view profit(s)? How do we reshape and restructure human values? The environmental crisis is only symptomatic of a larger problem of human values. Who do you love more, the Creator or the creation—the Giver or the gift? Who do you love more, people or profits?

The environmental crisis depicts a serious cultural lag—that is *our insatiable desire for things* is leading human spiritual development. Our abominable behaviors are destroying our national purpose and defiling the land we love. We must call to remembrance that we were established as *"one nation under God, indivisible, with liberty and justice for all."* For after all, justice is a spiritual concept based upon Jesus' two great commandments. "And Jesus answered him, The first of all commandments is, Hear, O Israel; The Lord our God is one Lord: And thou shalt love the Lord thy God with all thy heart, and with all thy soul, and with all thy mind, and with all thy strength: this is the first commandment. And the second is like, namely this, Thou shalt love thy neighbor as thyself. There is none other commandment greater than these" (Mark 12:29–31).

God and truth are synonymous. If we say that we are one nation under God, then we should act like children of God who are doing the works of God, who is our spiritual Father. But if we are doing abominable things to each other as well as to our natural environment, then we are doing the works of our earthly *father*, the devil (John 8:44). The devil is the spiritual father of this world. Thank God we are no longer under Mosaic Law. We are under the grace, mercy, and forgiveness of God through His only begotten Son, Jesus the Christ: the Righteous One.

Humankind obsessed with individual "material redemption" has developed numerous creature comforts: electric toothbrushes, shoe brushes, knives, hairbrushes, and so on. It's the philosophy of "I got mine you get yours." Of course, this is *animalism*, not human community. Hence, humankind has underdeveloped the one institution, the church, that God gave us for our own intellectual integrity and character development. There is nothing on the inside directing what individuals create on the outside: the environment. Life is about joy, peace, and happiness. But these mental states of being are born out of internal peace of mind and are then manifested outwardly as *harmony*.

A hurricane named "Super" Sandy in October 2012 was probably an expression of the environmental crisis we are now facing, an ungodly mindset toward the creation. This ecological crisis is caused by human beings failing to mentally and spiritually develop in accordance with the will of God expressed in the creation story: be fruitful, multiply, replenish and subdue the earth. That is, the failure of human beings to remember that the earth is the Lord's and the fullness thereof. The ecological crisis is indeed a spiritual values crisis—a monumental crisis of human values. This spiritual crisis causes human beings to create a *love affair with lies* rather than with the truth and love evil more than good, simply because the truth demands social cost accountability. A lie only requires abstract belief. *Believe the lie and the mental damage is done in the mind.* Good is good and evil is evil; and of course lies are only initiated to confuse the difference between truth and lies.

Exploitation as a value is institutionalized in our political processes, economic processes, educational processes, and social processes as a means of restricting access to valued societal resources. Our failure to integrate ideas is reflected in our inability to integrate cultures and so-called ethnic and racial categories. God says, I created all nations out of one-blood, and of course blood is red. To be sure, "flesh and blood cannot inherit the Kingdom of God" 1 Corinthians 15:50). Human exploitation is negativism to the *nth* degree. Human beings acting negatively toward self invariably causes negativism toward our natural habitat, the universe. Indeed it is inconsistent for people to talk about community and exploitation at the same time. Inconsistency (lies) breeds moral and ethical bankruptcy. Therefore, our greatest source of pollution is our mindset and the negative ideas that stem from our worldview. Hence, either/or logic and the negative assumptions that guide our theory construction and undergird our social structures are based upon extremes rather than the in-between. For after all, sometimes life is about the in-between rather than the extremes.

The following cross-classification table illustrates the point. For clarification purposes I shall provide heading definitions.

- Axiology refers to one's worldview: how humans view the world and their place in the scheme of things. What values drive a particular theory concerning the meaning of Life?
- Epistemology is the process by which individuals acquire knowledge and understanding.
- Logic refers to ways of reasoning (inductive/deductive) based upon the concepts of cause and effect.

AXIOLOGY	EPISTEMOLOGY	LOGIC
Man/Object	Cognition	Either/Or
Man/Nature	Co-native	Set Theory
Man/Man	Affective	Di-unity ("and" thinking)[1]

Increasingly, American society is being characterized by *scientism*, or a human-to-object approach to life rather than a human-to-human approach. Out of the notion that science is a cure-all, a technical culture has emerged, committed to a wholly materialistic style of life. Thus scientism has profoundly altered our natural habitat, the universe. Humankind's scientific orientation marks a change in the way we grasp the universe and our collective lives together. For after all, science is not God. God is the God of science as well. Embracing a worldview that defines *power* and values external to individuals is a dangerous zero-sum power game. Ways of societal organization reflect what societies think is the purpose and meaning of life. Obviously, life is not about human and environmental exploitation but human community, or *godly interdependence*. God has spoken to prophets in every generation; therefore God has not changed his theology from one generation to the next.

---

1   The concept of "and" in the spiritual context of this discussion means "spiral" thinking, rather than either/or thinking. "Either/or" thinking is about extremes, or polar opposites. "And" thinking is about finding the universal dimension in all things; therefore "and" thinking is more suitable to conflict resolution and problem solving. God is in the *center* of all things. The problem is the individual's ability to recognize the "and" factor. Jesus was an "and" thinker. This is why He could say to the crowd: "He that is without sin cast the first stone." The Mount of Transfiguration experience was about "and" thinking/communication. To be sure, either/or thinking invariably produces zero-sum-game thinking (*privilege*), rather than win-win thinking (*shared responsibility*). Life is not about extremes but the in-between, the center. "And" at the center of life is God.

The religion of Jesus cannot give rise to a value orientation that embraces a *worldview* that orients individuals toward the things of this world. Again, Christians are commanded to be in the world but not of the world. Without a doubt, the religion of Jesus was about godly stewardship, not material goodies. Human exploitation invariably creates waste, pollution, violence, and above all a loss of meaning and collective purpose. Individuals seeking to recreate through exploitation have created an unreal world and environmental chaos. The environmental crisis does not stem from a lack of technological knowledge; generating the appropriate technology is the least of our problems. Our spiritual-societal problem is that we have divided ourselves from ourselves. In fact, we have plenty to live on, but we are increasingly creating an environment whereby we have nothing to live for. The American dream is becoming the American nightmare. America needs to stand still and witness the salvation of the Lord: the works of God (Psalms 77). All *devils* do not operate in darkness; some operate in our families, our churches, our schools, and even more so in our hallowed governmental halls. Beware of the devils in all manmade places. Therefore, we have:

- Shootings in our city streets
- Schools that fail to educate our children
- Teachers who cannot teach
- Pastors who refuse to love and serve God's people, but self-serve
- Politicians who want the power to govern others, but have no self-spiritual governance power
- Children who are mechanized rather than spiritualized
- Fathers who are AWOL
- Mothers who are more concerned about what they put on their children rather than what they spiritually put in their children

All of this fleshly negativism adds up to a ball of societal confusion: vanity, vanity, and more vanity. "The moving finger writes and having writ moves on." But, what we have to look forward to as citizens of this great nation (the United States) and citizens of the world is: "And as it is appointed unto men once to die, but after this the judgment" (Hebrews 9:27). For it is certain: "we must all appear before the judgment seat of Christ; that everyone may receive the things done in his body, according to that he hath done, whether it be good or bad" (2 Corinthians 5:10). Therefore, without a doubt: "every one of us shall give in account of himself to God" (Romans 10:12). There are two sides in this spiritual fight: God's side versus the devil's side. Every individual has a choice. The author has chosen God's side.

In my opinion, four negative values have guided American affluence:

1. **Growth:** "the more the better" *and* "the bigger the better." This approach to life is the philosophy that materialism brings happiness. But God says, "A man's life does not consist in the abundance of the things which he possesses."

2. **Consumption:** the idea that consumption produces both progress and prosperity: *external values.*

3. **Technology:** more and better technology, and the notion that science is a cure-all. Indeed, *science* is not a magic bullet.

4. **Plentiful nature ethic:** the notion that nature is a free resource which is endless in scope. God is endless, not nature, because nature is not God.

Institutionalizing negativism/human exploitation has not facilitated two necessary processes for the development of community locally, nationally, and internationally:

1. **Integration of ideas.** If individuals cannot integrate ideas, then we will never integrate cultures and bodies. This is precisely why integrated education in our public school systems is so very important to our democratic way of life.

2. **Systems integration and systems analysis.** We need positive organizational change strategies or else hope is gone. Everything must change; nothing that is of human creation can ever remain the same.

American society and the world at large are indeed playing environmental death games—creating a culture of death rather than a culture (and world community) that embraces the fullness of life. The resolution to our current ecological crisis will require:

• Individuals as well as American society to become more responsible stewards (*godly stewardship*)

• Stewardship changes in our value orientations and institutional structures

Our collective sin is our ego-tripping desire to improve upon God's creation. In so doing, we are guilty of prideful, arrogant sensuality and above all self-withdrawal: seeking to serve our own ego interests. False pride brings about human tragedy, suffering, and death—symbolically, culturally, and physically. Increasingly, Americans are becoming void of ethical codes of conduct, especially in our national politics. The "thingification" of American culture is transforming the middle class and upper class into *no class*.

The void of ethical codes of conduct (inner motives) has disastrous modern technological consequences, especially for our food supply. Food shelf life has become "until someone buys it" because of chemical additives. This negative idea of *human exploitation* has placed us on the wrong side, fighting against God, natural laws, and even ourselves. Dinosaurs are extinct because of some type of environmental calamity. As humans, we are the endangered species because of our own greed, envy, and jealousy, and our exploitation and pollution of the environment for mammon: *money*. To be sure, natural resources are not unlimited. Therefore stewardship is called for. After all, one generation must plant the trees so that the next generation may reap the shade. Hence, the perpetuation of energy should be the universal currency, not money. Of course, America's inability to learn this profound lesson has produced an energy crisis as well as a self-imposed monetary crisis. Energy of some kind (wind, air, oil, gas, and coal) is needed for the production of all goods and services.

Alternative forms of technology are simply modernistic forms of *pietism*, rather than collective responsibility. Self-serving *greedy* individualism at the expense or exclusion of collective responsibility depicts the essence of the human predicament. Humankind is a slow learner because in almost two thousand years of Christian history we have not learned very much at all about life, God, or self. We all should ask ourselves: What time is it? The answer ought to be "it is God's time," because *God is time*. We therefore must find creative ways of getting the *truth* back into our politics and corporate structures in order to have a more perfect union. The founding fathers believed that the truths recorded in the Bible were the basis for a more perfect union in all aspects of our national life, both private and public. I concur with the founding fathers because the Bible is the book of life.

Our blatant immoral indifference toward the Word of God has landed us in the horrible mess we are in as a society. "If my people, which are called by my name, shall humble themselves, and pray, and seek my face, and turn from their wicked ways; then will I hear from heaven, and will forgive their sin, and will heal their land" (2 Chron. 7:14). *We have too many fence-straddling Christians.* Too many Christians do not understand who they are when they say they are "a Christian," which means "Christlike," or one who loves and serves others. This fence-straddling condition has some Christians with one foot in the church and one foot in the country club or nightclub, dancing, drinking, and letting the good times roll. That is, living as though there is no tomorrow and no spiritual accounting for deeds done in the flesh. "No one can serve two masters; for either he will hate the one and love the other, or he will hold to one and despise the other. You cannot serve God and mammon" (Matt. 6:24).

Clubbing and churching do not mix well, whether it is *country clubbing or nightclubbing*. For God is a jealous God. "I know your deeds, that you are neither hot nor cold; I would that you were cold or hot. So because you are lukewarm, and neither hot nor cold, I will spit you out of My mouth" (Rev. 3:15–16). As Christians we are to: "Be careful for nothing; but in everything by prayer and supplication with thanksgiving let your requests be made known unto God. And the peace of God, which passeth all understanding, shall keep your hearts and minds through Christ Jesus" (Phil. 4:6–7).

Trust me, as a Christian believer I am not being judgmental. *He that is without sin cast the first stone.* Jesus spoke these words to the crowd who wanted Him to give them permission to stone the woman to death that was accused of adultery. The spoken word and the written word are usually the same. Jesus probably wrote the same words in the sand. This book is simply an attempt to tell the truth, not throw rocks. We are all sinners, but glory to God, we have a salvation pathway named Jesus Christ. This is a clarion call for America to change direction: "Love ye one another as I have loved you." God has a sovereign will and He has a permissive will; even when we mess up God's grace and mercy are there to help us clean up. My honest plea is that as a society we get it together as one nation under God, indivisible, with liberty and justice for all. We need to heal our arbitrary divides so that we might be a light to the world community and indeed live by a constitution grounded in the solemn declaration that *we hold these truths to be self-evident, that all men are created equal.* In other words, a living social contract based upon godly spiritual truths.

Seemingly, there is an ungodly alliance between the super-rich Christian evangelicals that comprise the so-called Christian right and the corporate business structure. This alliance works to keep some Americans locked out and other Americans locked in. Being locked in or out produces similar results: confusion. Freedom is always the issue. God doesn't seem to be included in this social equation at all. God is a God of inclusion, not exclusion; we are all His children, equal in dignity before His throne. Before we were conceived in our mothers' wombs God knew us and even numbered the hairs that would be on our heads (Matt. 10:30). This kind of elitist, exclusionary thinking hurts everyone, both rich and poor, as well as those in between, that are middle class.

But, on the other hand: "A good man leaveth an inheritance to his children's children: and the wealth of the sinner is laid up for the just" (Prov. 13:22). In short, the riches of the wicked are stored up for the righteous. In this zero-sum game no one is a winner, especially America, because we have become politically polarized rather than spiritually unified. It is about right and wrong and justice and injustice, not partisan politics. As a consequence of all this moral confusion no one experiences the freedom that is in service to God, country, and fellowman.

This self-serving approach toward life creates confusion (lies), not a spiritually healthy society (nation-building initiatives). Institutionalizing lies creates not only confusion but inequalities. However, it does provide the manipulators of this approach with the arbitrary latitude to be evil rather than righteous. As Jesus said, "It is easier for a camel to go through the eye of a needle, than for a rich man to enter the kingdom of God" (Matt. 19:24). In my opinion, it would be too simplistic to describe this moral confusion as simply *human failure* when God says that the love of money is the root of all evil—that is, substituting money for God is evil. In fact, some people are so fearful of losing external physical control over societal resources that they fail to exercise control over *self*, the only entity that an individual can and should want to control. *Learning self-control is a monumental job in and of itself.*

For example, King David was a man after God's own heart, but he failed to control his sexual desire. His lust caused him to kill an innocent man in order to cover up his ungodly behavior (sin). King Solomon, the wisest man we know of historically, failed to control his lustful desires, and as a result he corrupted the Temple with *ungodly* women. Samson, the strongest man we know of historically, gave the secret of his *godly strength* to lustful Delilah. However, his strength was not in his hair but in his *obedience* to the will of God. His disobedience is what caused the loss of his *superman strength*, not Delilah cutting off his hair.

There are just some things an individual cannot do, namely disobey a direct order from God, and expect the power of God to remain in and with them. Job more than any other biblical character wrestled with the problems of evil, suffering, and social injustice. However, in the end Job declared: "Naked came I out of my mother's womb, and naked shall I return thither: the Lord gave, and the Lord hath taken away: blessed be the name of the Lord. In all of this, Job sinned not, nor charged God foolishly" (Job 1:21–22). The Bible declares that Job was an upright man who ran from sin, not toward sin. Through all his travails Job knew one thing: "The fear of the Lord is the beginning of wisdom: A good understanding has all those who do His commandments; His praise endures forever" (Ps. 111:10).

God gives everyone free will. However, not everyone is motivated to do the right thing. Therefore, societal *just* laws must be in place to refrain evildoers. Of course, our criminal justice system and civil codes are based upon the Ten Commandments (Judaism/Christianity). Indeed America is polarized. What then is the basis for the undercurrent fueling our national polarization? The political focus on the liberal-conservative dichotomy is unhealthy politically, but even more so governmentally. This condition has caused governmental paralysis in our national politics. Hence, the issues are right and wrong: inclusion versus exclusion. More importantly, the issues are the will of God versus the will of the devil. Motives on both sides are convoluted because of who is being included and who is being excluded (*inclusion versus exclusion*). God wants every person free to understand where your individual rights end and the other person's rights begin—and of course truly know the difference.

All of us should want what God precisely wants for each of us: "He hath shewed thee, O man, what is good; and what doth the Lord require of thee, but to do justly, and to love mercy, and to walk humbly with God" (Mic. 6:8). Unfortunately, some are willing to have nothing in order that others might have nothing, rather than everyone having something: heaven on earth. It is profoundly sad when individuals are willing to experience hell physically and then die and have their souls end up in hell.

GODLY LEADERSHIP

Are leaders born, made, or created? Both are God's workmanship created by Jesus Christ unto good works. "For we are his workmanship, created in Christ Jesus unto good works, which God hath before ordained that we should walk in them" (Eph. 2:10). America is in dire need of godly stewardship-oriented leadership in every sector of our national life: home, church, school, corporate/business structures, and governmental bodies. The leadership problem cannot be overemphasized. To be sure, church leadership has not changed very much over the centuries. Even during Jesus' lifetime many religious leaders preached a doctrine that condemned others but exalted themselves: Pharisees, Sadducees, scribes, and lawyers. These individuals tried to goad Jesus into saying something against Mosaic Law so they could stone Him to death, and of course they did succeed in stoning Stephen to death.

Jesus said, "Think not that I am come to destroy the law, or the prophets: I am not come to destroy, but to fulfill" (Matt. 5:17). All have sinned but one: *Jesus, Jesus, Jesus.* "This is a faithful saying, and worthy of all acceptation, that Christ Jesus came into the world to save sinners; of whom I am chief" (1 Tim. 1:15). Godly leadership in churches is central to the ushering in of a righteous society, because if church leadership is *morally upside down or double-minded*, then invariably society becomes twisted. The issue of leadership is one of *servant leadership versus self-serving leadership.*

Pastoral leaders and political leaders have formed an ungodly money alliance based upon "if you don't hold me accountable for my decisions/moral actions [*stealing*], then I will not hold you accountable for your decisions."

Many pastors attend seminaries and business schools to learn corporate business practices with an *eye* toward manipulating church resources for personal gain, not to learn how to rightly divide the word of truth. "Study to shew thyself approved unto God, a workman that needeth not be ashamed, rightly dividing the word of truth" (2 Tim. 2:15).

Many theologically untrained "storefront preachers" who declare that God *called them* organize churches with a few skilled individuals designed to serve them and them only. These types of churches have no internal accountability or external denominational accountability. They are simply one-person shows. The primary objective of these individuals is to access tax-free unaccountable monies. These preacher-leaders do not want educated individuals as a part of the church community: educated people ask too many accountability questions. In fact, these individuals in a New York minute will retort: "You need to start your own church. This is my church, and if you want to run a church, then go start one."

This is a statement of *ungodly* sentiments, not godly responsibility. Usually these churches have only a few members because of ungodly retorts made from the pulpit. No one was present when these preachers declared that they were called; therefore *what is it for a man to tell a lie?*

Without, a doubt, these preacher-leaders are yoking people by creating spiritual prisons (spiritual slavery). Only God can see motive because sin is housed in motive. God-fearing individuals must judge trees—that is judge individuals by the fruit they bear, or their works. This is the conclusion of the whole matter:

> Beloved, believe not every spirit, but try the spirits whether they be of God: because many false prophets are gone out into the world. Hereby know ye the Spirit of God: Every spirit that confesseth that Jesus Christ is come in the flesh is of God: And every spirit that confesseth not that Jesus Christ is come in the flesh is not of God: and this is that spirit of the anti-Christ, whereof ye have heard that it should come; and even now already is it in the world. Ye are of God, little children, and have overcome them: because greater is he that is in you, than he that is in the world. They are of the world: therefore speak of the world, and the world heareth them. We are of God: he that knoweth God heareth us; he that is not of God heareth not us. Hereby know we the spirit of the truth, and the spirit of error.
>
> Beloved, let us love one another: for love is of God; and everyone that loveth is born of God, and knoweth God. He that loveth not knoweth not God. He that loveth not knoweth not God; for God is love. In this was manifested the love of God toward us, because that God sent his only begotten Son into the world, that we might live through him. Herein is love, not that we loved God, but that he loved us, and sent his Son to be the propitiation for our sins.

Beloved, if God so loved us, we ought also to love one another. No man hath seen God at any time. If we love one another, God dwelleth in us, and his love is perfected in us. Hereby know we that we dwell in him, and he in us, because he hath given us his Spirit. And we have seen and do testify that the Father sent the Son to be the Savior of the world. Whosoever shall confess that Jesus is the Son of God, God dwelleth in him, and he in God. And we have known and believed the love that God hath to us. God is love; and he that dwelleth in love dwelleth in God and God in him.

Herein is our love made perfect, that we made have boldness in the Day of Judgment: because as he is, so are we in this world. There is no fear in love; but perfect love casteth out fear: because fear hath torment. He that feareth is not made perfect in love. We love him, because he first loved us. If a man says, I love God, and hateth his brother, he is a liar: for he that loveth not his brother whom he hath seen, how can he love God whom he hath not seen? And thiscommandment have we from him, That he who loveth God love his brother also.

1 John 4:1–21

My reason for quoting this lengthy scripture is this: as Christians we must understand our godly obligation to distinguish truth from false teaching. There is an awful lot of false doctrinal teaching and preaching taking place in churches today simply for congregational control. A lot of this false doctrinal teaching is by design for the things of the world. If unsound teaching and preaching is found in one Christian church, it is one too many. Again, get right, church: the King of Kings is coming! We are in the end times—not the end of the world, but the return of Jesus Christ for His church and a great spiritual awakening.

PRAYER

God, we know that You do not sleep or slumber for You are faithful to perfect Your will in us and through us as well as Your divine purposes for the world, especially America. Heavenly Father, You are a sovereign God and there is none other besides You; nothing is impossible for You. Therefore we give You all the glory, honor, and power. We pray that every American family, church leader, and political leader remember Your faithfulness in all things, because You work the nightshift. May we forever sing of Your forgiving mercy and loving-kindness unto us, generation after generation. We thank Thee for calling us into divine fellowship with You through Your Son Jesus Christ. Let the church be the church. Get right, church: the King of Kings is coming. Amen!

Chapter 6

GODLY SOCIETY VS. UNGODLY SOCIETY

Any society that does not embrace the Word of God is headed for a great fall. Great nations rise and great nations fall: the Egyptian empire, the Greek empire, and the Roman Empire. Obviously, the founding fathers believe this to be self-evident because of the slogan we place on our money: In God We Trust. America is not a theocracy and should not be a theocracy, but America is a great nation because it was founded upon biblical principles and doctrines. The spiritual tenets espoused are not advocating theocracy: *"We hold these truths to be self-evident that all men are created equal and endowed with certain inalienable rights from their creator."* This is simply an acknowledgment that our human rights come from God, not society. The world did not give human rights, but the world tries to take away human rights. "Peace I leave with you, my peace I give unto you: not as the world giveth, give I unto you. Let not your heart be troubled, neither let it be afraid" (John 14:27). God is simply saying, "I have your back as well as your front." In fact, God says, "I have you covered from the womb to the tomb." All we have to do as Christians is stand up.

Our humanity is grounded in the reality of God, who gave us divine free-will choice. Individuals have the right to be godly (wise) or devilish (foolish). We live in an electronic age characterized by endless writings of ungodly and devilish books; therefore much study has created a weariness of the flesh, which in turn promotes unbelief and separation of individuals from the reality of God. "The words of the wise are goads, and as nails fastened by the masters of assemblies, which are given from one shepherd. And further, by these, my son, be admonished: of making many books there is no end; and much study is a weariness of the flesh. Let us hear the conclusion of the whole matter: fear God and keep his commandments: for this is the whole duty of man. For God shall bring every work into judgment, with every secret thing, whether it be good or whether it be evil" (Eccl. 11:11–14).

Jesus further illuminates this same point: "But I say unto you, that every idle word that men shall speak, they shall give account thereof in the Day of Judgment. For by thy words thou shalt be justified, and by thy words thou shalt be condemned" (Matt. 12:36–37). Therefore the words that come forth from your own mouth will send you to heaven or hell. This is why we must show reverential fear of God and His Word as a controlling motive of life, in matters both spiritual and secular.

The Bible is the book of books and the eternal basis for godly living. "For verily I say unto you, Till heaven and earth pass, one jot or one tittle shall in no wise pass from the law, till all be fulfilled" (Matt. 5:18). *Jot* is the smallest letter in the Hebrew alphabet. A *tittle* is a small ornamental curl (horn) in Hebrew letters distinguishing one Hebrew letter from another. Therefore a *clarion call* is being issued to the church and church leadership to get right with God because time is running out. Let the church be the church of Jesus Christ, because Jesus is coming back for His church.

As humans we are born to be interdependent upon each other and to love and serve one another through the grace and knowledge of our Lord and Savior Jesus Christ. To Jesus Christ be the glory (2 Pet. 3:18). My prayer is that all men and women thank God for His eternal truth as we strive to become better Christians (godly) in loving and serving each other.

Death is the great spiritual equalizer; this includes both the good and the bad. Death does not respect cultural ethnicity, personhood, or economic status. The wages of sin is death. However, God made provisions for us not to be judged solely by our sins because of *Jesus the Christ;* and therefore God judges us on the good we could have done but left undone because of greed, envy, and jealousy. "For the wages of sin is death; but the gift of God is eternal life through Jesus Christ our Lord" (Rom. 6:23).

God is an awesome God, and He did not intend for individuals to live alone. "And the Lord God said, It is not good that man should be alone; I will make him a help meet for him" (Gen. 2:18). But we cannot live with each other unless we help each other; otherwise we have a dog-eat-dog philosophy. Hence, every individual must know their limitations so that they might be able to live in their expectations. This phrase is only applicable in the secular world. Christian believers know that all things are possible with God, who strengthens us through Christ Jesus.

Since the beginning of America (1619), Americans have been groping in the dark. To be sure though there is light on the horizon. "If we say that we have fellowship with him, and walk in darkness, we lie, and do not the truth: But if we walk in the light, we have fellowship one with another and the blood of Jesus Christ his Son cleanseth us from all sin" (1 John 1:6–7). Acknowledgment of this spiritual truth is based upon *faith*, because it is our *faith* that ultimately pleases God. However, we must recognize that the earth is the Lord's and the fullness thereof. Without a doubt, God is angry with the wicked. God saw fit to give us as human beings collective managerial authority over the earth and its natural resources, but we have failed to create just (godly) systems of sharing natural resources. This creates unnecessary ungodly conflict.

We are the United States of America. No individual state is greater than the sum total of *these United States of America.* To repeat the words of one of our greatest presidents: "A house divided against itself cannot stand." Social history in the twenty-first century should not repeat the mistakes of the past. If so the lives lost and the destruction of *things* this time can be far more devastating, and of course we may be conquered by an outside nation(s). The question is, is it wise to play with these types of *ungodly emotions* of the past? *Children who play with fire invariably get burned.* To be sure, biological maturity is not an insurance policy against mental immaturity. These types of graveyard emotions can ignite a firestorm that can destroy America. God gave Noah the rainbow as a sign that the earth will never be destroyed again by water (Gen. 9: 16–17). It will be fire the next time.

The sad state of affairs of evangelical Christian leadership is the same as it was in the past: rationalizing evil. It is not about a difference of *spiritual-political* opinions but the difference between what is right and what is wrong—*what is good and what is evil.* The question is raised; the decision and solution is up to each individual.

Together we stand and divided we fall. When we say fall what is being referenced is the end as we know it, and it shall never rise again! "If ye walk in my statutes, and keep my commandments, and do them; then I will give you rain in due season and the land shall yield her increase and the tree of the field shall yield their fruit" (Lev. 26:3–4). Conversely, "But if you will not hearken unto me, and will not do all of these commandments; and if ye shall despise my statutes, or if your soul abhor my judgments, so that ye will not do all my commandments, but that ye break my covenant: I also will do this unto you; I will appoint over you terror, consumption, and the burning ague, that shall consume the eyes, and cause sorrow of heart: and ye shall sow your seed in vain, for your enemies shall eat it" (Lev. 26:14–16).

God's law is the law, because God has the last word. "For whatsoever things were written aforetime were written for our learning, that we through patience and comfort of the scripture might have hope" (Rom. 15:4). We have God's divine grace, forgiveness, and truth and will not accept it; therefore we are in critical condition spiritually, and hope is on life support. Moreover, as a society, we certainly do not want Mosaic Law. "For the law was given by Moses, but grace and truth came by Jesus Christ" (John 1:17).

Indeed, Mosaic Law societies are failed, chaotic nation-states. Some nation-states in the Middle East are glaring examples of this. Jesus came to fulfill the law, not destroy the law. "Think not that I am come to destroy the law, or the prophets: I am not come to destroy, but to fulfill. For verily I say unto you, Till heaven and earth pass, one jot or tittle shall in no wise pass from the law, till all be fulfilled" (Matt. 5:17–18). As Christians, we are under God's grace, mercy, and truth because of Jesus Christ: the Righteous One. "For the law was given by Moses, but grace and truth came by Jesus Christ" (John 1:17). Therefore, these Mosaic Law advocates, under the guise of pretending to be working for the kingdom of God, are in fact working for the devil because their works fulfill the lusts of the devil and create confusion and self-righteousness, not God-centered righteousness.

Jesus hates hypocrites. "Ye hypocrites, well did Esaias prophesy of you, saying, This people draweth nigh unto me with their mouth, and honoureth with their lips; but their heart is far from me. But in vain they do worship me, teaching for doctrines the commandments of men"

(Matt. 15:7–9). On many occasions we fail to live up to the standards of the gospel. Backsling is very easy to do. In fact, *sometimes we can say we are Christian Right, but we just might be Christian Wrong.* The psalmist declares: "Thy word have I hid in mine heart, that I might not sin against thee" (Ps. 119:11). The book of Proverbs makes it even plainer by stating: "Every word of God is pure: he is a shield unto them that put their trust in him" (Prov. 30:5). "Knowest thou not this of old, since man was placed upon the earth, that the triumphing of the wicked is short, and the joy of the hypocrite but for a moment? Though his excellency mount up to the heavens, and his head reach unto the clouds; yet he shall perish forever like his own *dung:* they which have seen him shall say, where is he?" (Job 20:4–7).

"For God is not the author of confusion, but of peace, as in all churches of the saints" (1 Cor. 14:33). Indeed life is about individuals learning to live godly and holy lives, because holy is the Lamb of God that takes away the sins of the world. Sometimes people can fool themselves into believing they are good and doing the will of God, when they are in fact bad and doing the will of the devil (tricksters). In the name of God many individuals have been sent into war (religious crusades).

Nicodemus the Pharisee confronted Jesus with the question: *What must I do to be saved?* Jesus told him, "You are Jewish and know the law." Nicodemus answered by saying "all these things I have observed." Jesus replied, "One thing thou lack, you must be born again." (John 3:1–12). Observance of Mosaic Law will not get a person into heaven; therefore Mosaic Law is good but not good for you. It is the two great commandments of Jesus and being born again that afford an individual the opportunity to go to heaven (John 3:7). The Christian church must always take a godly stand against all forms of confusion, and the stand must be done decently and in order: *Love the sinner and hate the sin.* (1 Cor. 14:40). Too many individuals are obsessed with their individual wills and not God's will, because God's will is that we love each other as He loves us.

I must say that I commend the Catholic Church on its moral Christian consistency of belief. For example, the Catholic Church believes in the sanctity of life. Therefore, you should not take what you cannot give. Individuals cannot give life and therefore should not take a life. The Catholic Church is consistent in its belief concerning the death penalty and abortion. Human life belongs to God. Men seed life and women birth life into this world, but the origin of life is with God. Love the sinner and hate the sin. Without a doubt, sin is sin. Lying is sin. Fornication is sin. Adultery is sin. Homosexuality is sin. When society talks about rights in legalistic terms rather than moral terms; God is not in the mix. When individuals talk about morality then an absolute has to be the foundation of the discussion. God is the only absolute. God, then, is at the center of the discussion rather than humankind. When individuals talk about civil rights (*legalism*) the end game becomes relativism. We can take wrong and make it right and right and make it wrong (create confusion) and seem to make things work for a while. However, this flawed approach to life invariably creates chaos.

True Christianity is about setting a good example, both pastoral as well as parishioners. It's a twofold Christian responsibility.

The elders which are among you I exhort, who am also an elder, and a witness of the sufferings of Christ, and also a partaker of the glory that shall be revealed: Feed the flock of God which is among you, taking the oversight thereof, not by constraint, but willingly; not for filthy lucre, but of a ready mind; which neither as being lords over God's heritage, but being ensamples to the flock.

And when the chief Shepherd shall appear, ye shall receive a crown of glory that fadeth not away. Likewise, ye younger, submit yourselves unto the elder. Yea, all of you be subject one to another, and be clothed with humility: for God resisteth the proud, and giveth grace to the humble.

Humble yourselves therefore under the mighty hand of God, that he may exalt you in due time: Casting all your care upon him; for he careth for you. Be sober, be vigilant; because your adversary the devil, as a roaring lion, walketh about, and seeking whom he may devour: Whom resist steadfast in the faith, knowing that the same afflictions are accomplished in your brethren that are in the world.

But the God of all grace, who have called us unto his eternal glory by Christ Jesus, after that ye have suffered a while, make you perfect, stablish, strengthen, settle you. To him be glory and dominion forever. Amen. Greet ye one another with a kiss of charity. Peace be with you all that are in Christ Jesus. Amen.

1 Peter 5:1–11

Individuals should call to remembrance daily that: "The earth is the Lord's and the fullness thereof; the world, and they that dwell therein" (Ps. 24:1). If we are spiritually fruitful and multiply, replenish the earth as godlike caretakers, and as good stewards subdue the earth as God commanded, we have heaven on earth: because *everything* God made was very good. Amen. *Therefore do not take the earth off the climate change cliff!* Question: Why has everything good become bad? And a lot of things that were once bad are now good? Maybe the answer lies in the fact that as a nation we have forgotten that one generation plants the trees and the next generation reaps the shade. It just may be that the previous generation cut down too many trees, and therefore the sun is turning the land we love into a desert.

As Christians we are commanded to embrace *absolute commitment to Jesus Christ*. Jesus says, "I know your works, that thou art neither cold nor hot: I would thou wert cold or hot. So then because thou art lukewarm, and neither hot nor cold, I will spue thee out of my mouth" (Rev. 3:15–16). With Jesus there is no in-between position. "And when he had called the people unto him with his disciples also, he said unto them, whosoever will come after me, let him deny himself, and take up his cross, and follow me. For whosoever will save his life shall lose it; but whosoever shall lose his life for my sake and the gospel's, the same shall save it. For what shall it profit a man, if he shall gain the whole world, and lose his own soul?" (Mark 8:34–36).

Jesus called for total obedience to God's original intention for the world. Moreover, Jesus calls for a radical reversal of the world's value orientation of profit(s) and a revolutionary return to God's purpose for human life. Jesus says: "Behold, I stand at the door, and knock: If any man hears my voice, and opens the door, I will come in to him, and will sup with him, and he with me. To him that over cometh will I grant to sit with me in my throne, even as I also overcame, and am set down with my Father in his throne. He that hath an ear, let him hear what the Spirit saith unto the churches" (Rev. 3:20–22).

Jesus was not satisfied with a slice of the pie of *obedience*; He demands total obedience to the will of God. In fact, Jesus did not rejoice in the tithe of a big offering as much as He did in the sacrificial giving of a widow woman. Unfortunately, today we spend a disproportionate amount of time and resources on feelings (emotions) and too little time on faith and obedience. As a result, we have fostered a self-indulgent, do-your-own-thing culture, and the societal confusion is charged to our children.

Faith pleases God and obedience to God's will pleases Jesus. Indeed it is soul-searching time in America. We must slow our social roll before we destroy each other with secular "do your own thing" foolishness. Embracing the pleasure principle at any societal cost is collective societal suicide. "If it feels good do it" is not good because righteousness exalts a nation and sin is a reproach to God.

NEWTOWN IS YOUR TOWN, AMERICA

Our secular trinity (theology-sociology-psychology) has become so morally distorted that guns are now controlling us rather than individuals controlling guns. We have created a love affair with guns rather than God. The gun has become the source of power rather than truth. Until a man can make a human being out of the clay beneath his feet, and blow breath into his nostrils, he should not cavalierly kill a man. Therefore guns, like suicide, represent a permanent solution to temporary problems. When individuals choose a gun as a solution they are playing God. Life and death is a God issue; even the devil has to get permission from God.

The story of God, the devil, and Job is a prime example. Since individuals cannot give life, why then take what you cannot give? Once an individual kills another individual, "sorry" becomes a sorry word. Of course, there are other societal ills than guns, but the horrific societal downside is the attitudinal affect that the *gun culture* has on the nation's children, who grow up believing that the best way to resolve values conflicts is violently rather than non-violently.

Telling each other "little white lies" and killing each other does not solve socio-spiritual problems; it only exacerbates existing socio-spiritual problems. Therefore guns are not a solution, only an impediment to solving socio-spiritual problems (dysfunctional human interaction). A gun cannot kill the devil; therefore one individual killing another does not solve the spiritual-cultural problems in society. To be sure, there are those who speak boldly of the right to own a gun (Second Amendment), but what about an individual's First Amendment rights to life, liberty, and the pursuit of happiness?

Question: Do we as a nation, given weapons of mass destruction, really want to live by a strict interpretation/implementation of the Second Amendment? Implications: Strap it on, get it on! This type of mentality fuels the notion that a gun provides security (a false sense of security), because at the same time this type of mentality fuels eye-hand coordination with practice (wild, Wild West). This culturally uncivilized process is the epitome of societal insanity: the gun culture versus the moral culture. Those who desire a Second Amendment with no restrictions desire social/immoral chaos.

Twenty primary children in Newtown, CT, losing their precious lives in the mass shooting of 2012 ought to open our moral eyes, especially the moral eyes of the Christian church. One of the greatest theological treatises of the modern era is the "Letter from the Birmingham Jail" written by Dr. Martin L. King Jr to clergymen. The letter was written during the civil rights era of the 1960s. Christian clergyman were hypocritical of Dr. King stirring up confusion and upsetting the status quo of Governor George Wallace's declaration of "segregation now, segregation forever," because there are those who would rather learn to exist in a state of confusion, rather than seek to change the condition(s). Dr. King was simply saying to clergymen: "*I'm in jail, but I'm free.* You are physically free but enslaved to sin (wrongdoing). By accepting sin your mind (soul) is in chains. Therefore, you have learned how to be a happy slave to sin." Of course, there is no such state of existence as a happy slave. This is not the will of God.

Dr. King's reply to these clergymen was simply this: "If you were preaching and teaching the Bible based upon the gospel of Jesus Christ, you would be in jail with me." My exhortation to pastoral leaders is simply this: "If you were preaching and teaching the Bible based upon the Gospel of Jesus Christ, then we would not have a gun culture, but a Jesus culture." In fact, we would have a Jesus culture based upon the question: *What would Jesus do?* For after all, what about the First Amendment rights of twenty precious primary children in Newtown?

THE AFTERMATH OF THE 2012 ELECTION: WHICH WAY, AMERICA?

Since the Civil Rights era (1964–1965) of President Johnson, American society has steadily marched toward societal polarization over equal access to valued societal resources. In 2008, with the election of President Obama, the polarization crystallized. With the reelection of President Obama the notion of ethnic entitlement took a backseat to the concept of economic opportunity in society. In other words, leadership qualifications should not embrace cultural ethnicity. All Americans can succeed if they are willing to work hard, play by the rules, obey the laws of society, and understand self-sacrifice.

Therefore, the 2012 presidential election depicted an America at a crossroads, plagued by a declining middle class; a disinherited poor underclass; decaying infrastructures in our cities; environmental pollution; the moral dilemma of two unfunded wars; cultural exclusivism; an evangelical "Christian Right" religious leadership that is morally indifferent to ethnic-cultural changes and the needs of the poor; the spiritual-moral breakdown of the family; the spiritual inability of individuals to forgive one another; a loss of national purpose; and above all a super-rich class that seemingly believes they should have it all when they already own up to 80 percent of the nation's wealth. But most of all America is plagued by the corruption in our political system resulting from corporate money, which has made the country almost ungovernable. Combine this social fact with the rampant, pervasive, and unyielding moral corruption in our society; the rise of an unelected, one-man, no-increase-in-taxation doctrine fueled by the Tea Party's doctrine of austerity; and an unforgiving Southern confederate doctrine—and what you have is mass moral confusion. It even appears these forces are willing to destroy America.

To understand the historical context that has led us to the dilemma we now face as a nation, one must understand the history of America's development. Historically, in American society we have always lived the contradiction of *freedom and slavery*. Today the contradiction is not as glaring as in the historic past; however, to some degree it still exists. Obviously, laws can be legislated to address the issue, but morality cannot be legislated. Morality is housed in the spiritual dimensions of individual conscience, family life, and Christian doctrine. The spiritual brokenness in the Christian church community is magnified to the *nth* degree in our families as well as the society in general.

Blacks and other ethnic minorities have a God-given human right as well as a constitutional right to live and prosper in America from their own labor and ingenuity. No matter what the color, God says we are brothers and that we should love and serve one another as He loves and serves us. Clearly, God "hath made of one blood all nations of men for to dwell on all the face of the earth, and hath determined the times before appointed, and the bounds of their habitation; that they should seek the Lord, if haply they might feel after him, and find him, though he be not far from every one of us: For in him we live, and move, and have our being; as certain also of your own poets have said, for we are also his offspring" (Acts 17:26–28).

The only reason why this is not the norm (at this time) is because of institutional obstacles perpetuated primarily by some individuals of European descent—in spite of the fact that we are a nation of immigrants, based upon universal citizenship. Too many Europeans see skin color before they see the individual, especially in America, and particularly in the southeastern parts of the United States. Dr. Martin Luther King Jr. stated, "Individuals should be judged by the content of their character, not the color of their skin." The scriptural basis for Dr. King's statement is found in the Gospel of Matthew: "Ye have heard that it was said by them of old time, Thou shalt not kill; and whosoever shall kill shall be in danger of the judgment: But I say unto you, That whosoever is angry with his brother without a cause shall be in danger of the judgment: and whosoever shall say to his brother, Raca, shall be in danger of the council: but whosoever shall say, Thou fool, shall be in danger of hell fire" (Matt. 5:21–22). Also, I might add, these color-conscious Europeans are assisted by some ethnic minorities in leadership positions who desire things at the expense of their own moral values and intellectual integrity.

The United States of America is the most intellectually sophisticated technological society on planet Earth; therefore, after 394 years as a multicultural society, we should be able to call a timeout regarding exclusionary foolishness. Individuals from every nation-state on the planet yearn to come to America because doctrinally we include rather than exclude.

If we are not careful as a nation, we will find ourselves on the wrong side of human history, bordering on self-annihilation. This is because: "Blessed is the nation whose God is the Lord; and the people whom he hath chosen for his own inheritance" (Ps. 33:12). What is it that makes America exceptional? Is it the notion of universal God-given human rights? For after all, based upon the U.S. Constitution, we try to understand where one person's rights end and the other person's rights begin! Of course, our nation has not always been successful, because no human instrument is perfect; there are always some issues left open for interpretation. In some instances, interpretation of the law can be purchased by the highest bidder(s) and brutally enforced through the establishment.

Currently, a dangerous *uncivil* civil war is being waged in our nation based upon lies. Too many leaders do not want to be accountable for their policy decisions. Children of children always tell "little white lies." Children of God tell the truth every time, all the time, because God is time.

Can institutional Christianity become an honest moral broker for God and the kingdom of heaven? Can the Christian church be the God-centered light that strengthens the spiritual-moral fabric of our nation? Can the Christian church help a mega-rich man get to heaven, since it is easier for a camel to go through the eye of a needle than for a rich man to go to heaven? To conclude this matter: "But if ye will not do so, behold, ye have sinned against the Lord: and be sure your sin will find you out" (Num. 32:23). Of course, this is true for the rich as well as the poor. The point here is that the church is duty-bound to help everyone get to the kingdom of heaven.

The reelection of President Barack Obama clearly represented the following choice for our nation at a pivotal crossroads: *"One nation under God with liberty and justice for all."* This profound statement should be a way of life and not just a philosophical slogan. The social and demographic changes reflected in the results of the 2012 presidential election require a rethinking of our social and political processes—that is how we bring everyone into the socio-political-economic equation. No individual left behind. No family left behind. Get right, church. Let's go home. Straighten up America: fly right. The presidential election of 2008 was a moment in history. But the presidential election of 2012 must initiate a spiritual movement of justice for all, spearheaded by the Christian church, simply because justice is a spiritual concept. God is the righteous judge: He will judge us all, including the quick and the dead.

One day with man is like unto a thousand years with the Lord. "All scripture is given by inspiration of God, and is profitable for doctrine, for reproof, for correction, for instruction in righteousness: That the man of God may be perfect, thoroughly furnished unto all good works"

(2 Tim. 3:16–17). To be sure, "it is appointed unto men once to die, but after this, the judgment" (Heb. 9:27). Each and every American is a stakeholder in fostering the common good. America is headed over the immorality cliff whereby any and everything is acceptable as long as it increases the economic bottom line.

America should always stand for "one man: one vote." Therefore, man up. We need a societal prayer break based upon a "come to Jesus" moment: a national day of prayer for the spiritual healing of our nation, and we pray that this day shall last eternally in the hearts and minds of Americans. For "If my people, which are called by my name, shall humble themselves, and pray, and seek my face, and turn from their wicked ways; then will I hear from heaven, and will forgive their sin, and will heal their land" (2 Chron. 7:14). Hence, we humbly pray, world without end.

The overwhelming contributing factor toward the reelection of President Barack Obama was the Supreme Court's decision to uphold the healthcare bill as settled righteous law. Republicans made so-called "Obamacare" the centerpiece of their efforts to deny President Obama a second term and therefore make him a one-term president. Of course, if this labeling of the healthcare bill rings true it will transcend time as a legacy to the health and well-being of all Americans. At the presidential signing of the healthcare bill, Vice President Biden remarked to the president: "This is a big deal." And of course, it was a big deal! Simply because *thirty-eight million* Americans have access to affordable healthcare, and health is wealth.

Republicans were overconfident in their desire to defeat President Obama, and at the same time they felt confident that the healthcare law would be overturned because of a conservatively oriented U.S. Supreme Court coupled with high unemployment. Many Americans may differ with this political opinion; this is simply my analysis of what happened in President Obama's reelection.

Again, in my opinion, there are two contentious, emotionally charged moral issues confronting Americans. It is not jobs. We can easily solve the jobs problem if individuals in Congress of good will and common sense would simply choose to do so. Unfortunately, common sense is not always common. The jobs problem is not a philosophical problem. Work is a commandment from God. Work is a divine principle, and therefore work is God's gift to every human being. The jobs problem has become a hard-line political party problem.

The abortion and same-sex marriage issues are morally wrong in the sight of God. These issues are individual, moral conscience issues as well as societal and political issues. Of course, the devil does not know your personal business until you tell someone. Therefore, the devil just might be who you *tell*, because if an individual cannot keep his or her own secret(s), how then can you expect someone else to keep your secret(s)?

The Bible says that a person shouldn't let his left hand know what his right hand is doing. Keep your personal business to yourself. However, God is not fooled; He knows everything. Nothing is hidden from God. But God Himself gave every individual free will, and therefore as individuals we should be tolerant of the choices of others—while not accepting of the sin of others or participating in the sin of others. As individuals we have a free-will choice to go to heaven or hell. Therefore individuals should not seek to incorporate others into their sin. Publicly demonstrating (flaunting) sin should not be societally acceptable. We have moved beyond moral bankruptcy; we are in the age of no moral compass (conscience) at all. Any and everything goes, even to the degree of legalizing sin. No one knows what goes on behind closed doors with consenting adults until you tell someone; the devil does not even know.

Every opportunity God gives me to vote against and talk against sin, as a Christian I am duty-bound to do so, even my own sin. Sin is sin and God hates sin. "God judgeth the righteous, God is angry with the wicked every day" (Ps. 7:11). Tolerance does not require third-party participation or consent.

Today, when you get right down to it, the reason why there is so much confusion and discord in American society is because of the confusion in places of Christian worship—and above all because of the church's failure to be the conscience of our souls, hearts, and minds. In short, the Christian church has never lived up to its creed. Even during the lifetime of Jesus houses of worship were corrupted by money, power, and confusion. Jesus brought some order to houses of worship. The apostle Paul brought extensive order to the church because of his Damascus road experience.

The seedbed for this confusion is the desire of Christian churches for membership and worldly power, rather than the teaching of godly principles and doctrines. Without a doubt, the corruption in the church has spilled over into the political arena with its own particular brand of ungodly doctrine that declares "get the money, get the money, any kind of way get the money." To a profound degree the church does not preach/teach against societal corruption. The devil is corrupting the world and everything in it. In fact, the degree of corruption in the world is in direct proportion to the level of influence given to the devil by leadership and individuals in general. *Love* is the degree to which individuals are willing to share with each other. Corruption is the flipside of the coin: *sin*.

Likewise, the church does not profoundly preach/teach justice for all. Since, as we stated earlier, Sunday morning is still the most segregated time in American society, we must conclude that the Christian church does not believe in justice for all or the philosophy of love thy neighbor as thyself—in essence, trying to live within the framework of the Ten Commandments. The Ten Commandments represent God's will for individuals who desire to live a righteous life before Him.

Unfortunately, you will find unrighteousness in every institution in our society, including some Christian churches. And it is not getting better, but worse day by day. Get right, church, before it's too late. Let's climb Jacob's ladder to heaven rather than climb the world's ladder to hell. Every round with God goes higher and higher. But with the devil influencing the world, every round on the world's ladder descends lower and lower into the immoral abyss of "nothingness." Relativism is the devil's personal playground. Heaven's ladder takes us higher in the fruits of the Spirit: love, peace, joy, longsuffering, gentleness, goodness, faith, meekness, and temperance. The church is duty-bound to live in the fruits of the Spirit rather than the fruits of the flesh. Amen!

PRAYER

Heavenly Father, we pray for peace on earth and goodwill toward all. For every individual must come to know that Your body is the temple of the Holy Ghost, which is in us all, and we must all understand that we are not our own. For we were bought with a price: the life, blood, resurrection, and ascension of Jesus. Therefore, we must glorify our bodies and spirits which are of God (make no mistake about it: God owns us body and soul).

America needs every individual to become the best citizen that he or she can be. We ask that You fill each of us with a spirit of who Jesus is so that we might include others rather than exclude others. Help us to avoid the crippling effects of negativism and greed so that we might be able to change self, in order that we might love others rather than seek to control others. Give us the spirit of godly confidence that we can believe in each other as Americans and in the values of social democracy, but most of all believe in You, Almighty God. For indeed You have mightily blessed America, and now America must bless You, God our heavenly Father. Let the church be the church. Get right, church. Let's go home. Amen!

Conclusion

GOD'S FOURFOLD FOUNDATION FOR HEAVEN ON EARTH

Righteousness exalts a nation, but sin is shameful, spiritually stunting, contagious and disgraceful to any people if left untreated by God's Truth. "Thy word have I hid in mine heart, that I might not sin against thee. Blessed art thou, O lord: teach me thy statutes" (Psalm 119:11–12). However, God says, "If My people who are called by My name, shall humble themselves, and pray, and seek my face, and turn from their wicked ways; then will I hear from heaven, and will forgive their sins, and will heal their land" (2 Chron. 7:14)." This is the only way we can have a righteous society and at the time individuals learn how to climb Jacob's ladder to heaven. Unfortunately, we have strayed from the mainline and we need to get Jesus on the mainline in our institutional churches. God also says "My people perish for lack of vision and knowledge." For "Where there is no vision, the people perish: but he that keepeth the law, happy is he" (Proverbs 29:18). To reiterate, the fourfold foundation for heaven on earth is plainly stated:

- **Be fruitful of the spirit, not the flesh.** We are to magnify the fruits of the Holy Spirit (Gal. 5:22).
- **Multiply**. Marriage is God's spiritual command, not mankind's fleshly idea. God is not in the midst of same-sex marriage. Two men cannot multiply. Two women cannot multiply. Only a man and a woman can multiply. The way of the world is the enemy of God; and of course marriage is of God.
- **Replenish**. We must harvest, but we must also plant. We must sow and we must also reap.
- **Subdue**. Subdue refers to mankind keeping everything under godly influence and control, including self. Men should not seek to subdue women with money. Women should not seek to subdue men with sexuality.

The earth is our natural habitat—that is, our natural heaven on earth, not some foreign planet. Hence, God desires that the earth function as our natural physical heaven because He has a spiritual heaven for our souls that is not made by human hands. But, of course, the devil has a spiritual hell for our souls, even while we physically live on earth. However, if we submit ourselves to God and resist the wiles of the devil, he will flee from us as we run like hell from him. God desires pastoral leaders that love people and serve people, not pastoral leaders who exchange God's purpose for their personal gain. The keys to the kingdom of God are recorded in the Bible. Let the institutional church be the church of Jesus Christ, our Lord and Savior. God has *this* and *that* in His hands; He has the whole world in His hands. Let the institutional church say amen—world without end!